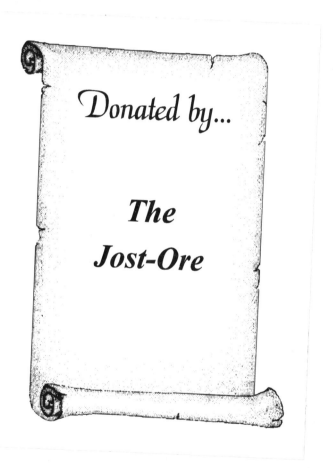

Congreve

Buffalo
July,
1981

" ... to nothing
and to no
one." P. 70
But bless those
special pairs.

Plays & Playwrights Series

EDITORS

Kenneth Richards & Peter Thompson

Harold Love

Congreve

ROWMAN AND LITTLEFIELD
Totowa, New Jersey

First published in the United States 1975
by Rowman and Littlefield, Totowa, N.J.

© Basil Blackwell 1974

Library of Congress Cataloging in Publication Data

Love, Harold, 1937–
  Congreve.

  (Plays & playwrights series)
  Bibliography: p.
  Includes index.
  1. Congreve, William, 1670–1729—Criticism and interpretation.

PR3367.L6   1975   822'.4   74–23234

ISBN 0–87471–623–3

Printed and bound in Great Britain by
The Camelot Press Ltd, Southampton

Contents

Preliminary Note

Congreve's plays are quoted in the text of Herbert Davis (Chicago: University of Chicago Press, 1967), and the line numbers hold good for this edition only, though they should give a rough indication of the position of passages in other editions which preserve the scene divisions of the original quartos.

Some modern texts follow the collected edition of 1710 in which the number of scene divisions was greatly increased. For these both the line and the scene numbers given in this book are likely to be misleading. To identify the original scene divisions it is necessary to locate the points at which there is an actual change of scenery. I have tried as far as possible to supplement act, scene and line references with more general indications of the whereabouts of passages in their respective plays.

H. L.

I

The Dramatist
and his Theatre

William Congreve was born in Yorkshire in 1670, the son of an army officer who became the steward to an Irish earl, and educated at Kilkenny school and Trinity College, Dublin, at both of which he was briefly a contemporary of Swift. His importance as a writer rests on five plays produced in London between 1693 and 1700, the last when he was only thirty. The rest of his life, which ended in 1729, was spent in sociable indolence supported by the proceeds of commissioner-ships for wine and for licensing hackney coaches which brought him in £100 a year, and, from 1714, the much more valuable sinecure of Secretary to the Island of Jamaica (which he never, of course, had to visit in person).

Most of what is known of his private life can be found in two admirably thorough but rather unexciting books by the late John C. Hodges, *William Congreve, the Man* (1941) and *William Congreve: Letters and Documents* (1964). The lack of excitement is not Hodges' fault; Congreve's life, or that part at least which has been recorded for us, was a singularly uneventful one. He experienced none of the dizzying reversals of fortune which signalize the careers of the other masters of Restoration comedy, Wycherley, Etherege, Farquhar, and Vanbrugh, nor does he reveal himself in his non-dramatic writings as vividly as Wycherley in his poems (despite their badness), Etherege in his astute and amusing diplomatic correspondence, or Farquhar in his cheeky forays into criticism. From the testimony of Congreve's friends, we gain the impression of an amiable hedonist who complained about his weight, his gout, and his poor eyesight, yet in his forties

was still able to win the heart of the bluestocking Duchess of Marlborough, and at fifty-three to father a child by her. It has also been
pointed out to his credit that in an age of endemic poetical backbiting
he seems to have been on excellent terms with most of his fellow-
writers, including those who disagreed with his politics: the Tory
Pope was to pay the Whig Congreve the very great honour of making
him dedicatee to the translation of *The Iliad*.

Beyond these general impressions, there is not much that a study
of the life has to offer a reader of the plays. The reticence which
Congreve prized so much in Mirabell and whose neglect he pilloried
in Tattle made it certain that anything compromising to others in
his private history would be scrupulously kept to himself. However,
if Congreve the man eludes us, Congreve the writer is excellently
placed for our consideration. His plays survive in good texts; we
know a great deal about the theatre for which they were written;
and most important of all we can still see them today. *The Way of the
World* and *Love for Love* are among the most frequently revived of
non-Shakespearean classical plays and even *The Double Dealer* and
The Old Batchelour will occasionally surface among amateurs. His
tragedy, *The Mourning Bride*, has not enjoyed a twentieth century
revival nor does it seem very likely to, but in 1970 the opera *Semele*,
in Handel's setting, could be seen in London in a handsome production
by the Sadler's Wells company.

Some playwrights are content to be thought of as artists in the
theatre; others like to feel that they are contributing to literature
and that their works deserve to be judged by literary canons. Congreve
was definitely of the second kind. His dedications and critical essays
lay great stress on what he saw as the literary excellences of his plays
and have virtually nothing to tell us about how they were performed.
When he reprinted the plays in 1710 he reorganized the layout of the
text according to the French and Roman system by which a new
scene begins every time there is an entrance or an exit, apparently
with the aim of making it look more like an edition of a literary
classic, and less like a script. Given his meticulous concern with niceties
of style, it is quite likely that he would have agreed with his friend
and mentor Dryden that it was the 'propriety of thought and words'
which was the essential beauty of a play and that this was 'but con-
fusedly judged in the vehemence of action'.[1] Such things should

---

[1] Dedication to *The Spanish Friar* (1681) in *Of Dramatic Poesy and Other Critical
Essays*, ed. George Watson (London, 1962), I, 278.

caution us against too narrow a theatrical approach to Congreve, yet at the same time it would be foolish for us to ignore the fact that the plays did begin their lives as scripts and that even in 1710 most of their readers would already have seen them acted.

It would be an act of even more sublime folly (and yet one to which some very distinguished critics have been party) to demand the same fullness of realization of the text of a comedy one does of that of a poem or novel. A novel exists in its completeness on the page. A written play is complete only when it is projected out from the page into space and time, and readers of Congreve, even those who are not particularly interested in the theatre, must be prepared to make allowance for this. The most elementary point, but one that can still somehow be overlooked, is that the words which go to make up Congreve's dialogue are units of sound as well as meaning. He writes to be spoken and more particularly to be spoken to a certain kind of hearer in a certain kind of building. He is conscious of the sonorities of the human voice in exactly the same way as a musician writing a violin concerto has to be conscious of those of the violin. We cannot know whether he followed the recommendation of his friend Charles Gildon that playwrights should pronounce their dialogue as they composed it, imitating 'the Voice and Utterance' of the character concerned,[2] but we have the word of Kenneth Muir that 'every actor whether amateur or professional' with whom he has discussed the matter agrees 'that after acting in Congreve they find all other dramatic prose inferior and more difficult to deliver effectively'.[3] It follows that when we read him we also need to hear him—and not just to hear him passively but to test his lines vocally in search of the emphasis and inflection which is exactly right for them. To read him in the unvocal way we read a novel is to misconceive his art in a quite crucial way.

I feel it necessary to stress the importance of an active aural imagina-tion to an understanding of Congreve because it is something that is increasingly foreign to our own habits, especially if we have fallen victim to the speed-readers. However, with a play, it is not enough to hear; it may also be very important that we see or at least spatialize what we read. The dramatist conceives his play for a physical medium and his script by itself will rarely supply all the information necessary

[2] Charles Gildon, *The Complete Art of Poetry* (London, 1718), I, 258.
[3] 'Congreve on the Modern Stage', in *William Congreve*, ed. Brian Morris (London: Benn, 1972), p. 150.

to grasp that conception. Playwrights of Congreve's generation were in close contact with their actors and their audiences and saw no need for elaborate stage-directions. Fortunately they will often compensate for this by incorporating descriptions of what is being presented into the dialogue. Thus we have no difficulty in picturing the physical movement which is the real dramatic point of this speech of Almeria from *The Mourning Bride*; indeed we could even argue that the lines are little more than a series of cues to the performer as to what she should be doing vocally and physically:

> *Almeria.* O, I am struck; thy Words are Bolts of Ice,
> Which shot into my Breast, now melt and chill me.
> I chatter, shake, and faint with thrilling Fears.
> No, hold me not—O, let us not support,
> But sink each other, lower yet, down, down,
> Where levell'd low, no more we'll lift our Eyes,
> But prone, and dumb, rot the firm Face of Earth
> With Rivers of incessant scalding Rain.
>
> [III.i.367–74]

It is our good fortune that even in comedy Congreve was fairly conscientious about giving this kind of help to his performers and thus also to his readers; however, there are still passages where we have to make do as well as we can without it. Take for instance, from *The Way of the World*, Lady Wishfort's rehearsal for her reception of Sir Rowland:

> *Lady Wishfort.* Will he be
> Importunate *Foible*, and push? For if he shou'd not be
> Importunate————I shall never break Decorums————I
> shall die with Confusion, if I am forc'd to advance————Oh
> no, I can never advance————I shall swoon if he shou'd
> expect advances. . . . I won't be too coy neither.————I
> won't give him despair————But a little Disdain is not
> amiss; a little Scorn is alluring.
> *Foible.* A little Scorn becomes your Ladyship.
> *Lady Wishfort.* Yes, but Tenderness becomes me best————A
> sort of a dyingness————You see that Picture has a sort of
> a————Ha *Foible*? A swimminess in the Eyes————Yes, I'll
> look so————My Niece affects it; but she wants Features.
>
> [III.i.156–70]

This is a good example of a scene conceived in terms which are primarily physical and only secondarily verbal. Its real substance is not what Lady Wishfort says, but her experiments with accent and posture as she says it, and until we have recomposed the scene physically we can not be said to have read it.

It will also be helpful in attempting to see Congreve's scenes as he himself would have seen them if we know something of the performers for whom he wrote, especially the three greatest of them, Elizabeth Barry, Anne Bracegirdle, and Thomas Betterton. Synge said in the Preface to *The Playboy of the Western World* that all art was a collaboration. He was thinking when he said it of the language of drama as being a gift to the dramatist from those who speak it, but another kind of dramatist might easily have felt exactly the same thing about his performers in that it was in terms of their voices, their movements, and their powers, tested and potential, that his play was first conceived. It is hardly outrageous, for instance, to claim that Shakespeare was able to create Hamlet only because Richard Burbage was ready to act a Hamlet, and that if he had been writing the play with another actor in mind it would have been another kind of play and, if a lesser actor, probably a lesser play.

Congreve was not an actor and despite his long and close personal relationship with Anne Bracegirdle is unlikely to have shaken off a sense of being their social superior. (There was no suggestion of his marrying her.) But he will have known them and their abilities probably as well as they could be known by someone who had not actually trodden a stage with them. As a playwright he will have had to perform several functions which might now be regarded as falling in the province of the producer, among them that of reading the script aloud to the performers and instructing them in the 'humours' of their parts and how particular lines were to be pronounced. (This last was taken very seriously indeed: Betterton once gave a man money for recalling for him the intonation of a line in a performance by Charles Hart.) It should also be kept in mind that from 1681 until 1695 there was only one company active in London; in fact it must have been difficult for dramatists who knew the repertoire only from the performances of this company *not* to tailor parts to the talents of its members. The professional playwrights were quite explicit in their attention to this; it was an essential part of their trade. John Dennis, writing in 1711, even went as far as to claim that 'Most of the Writers for the Stage in my time, have not only adapted their

Characters to their Actors, but those Actors have as it were sat for them.'[4] The principle involved was that most succinctly put fifty years after Congreve's death by Mozart when he wrote to his father 'I like an aria to fit a singer as perfectly as a well-made suit of clothes.'[5] Congreve had seen plays at the Smock Alley theatre in Dublin but the main part of his education in theatre was acquired from the very performers whom he went on to clothe in parts that were perfectly measured to their talents. When in 1695 the stars of the United company led by Betterton left Drury Lane to set up on their own at Lincoln's Inn Fields, Congreve came with them as sharer and house dramatist and provided them with their two greatest triumphs in *Love for Love* and *The Mourning Bride*. Given this closeness of dramatist to performers, it is no denigration of Congreve to suggest that the greatness of the comedy owed something to the greatness of the actors and actresses, or at the very least that if they had not been there to perform, he would not have been inspired to write so superbly.

That they were great is beyond doubt. Their reputations cast a spell of suspended development over a whole half-century of the English theatre. Their interpretations were carefully passed down from performer to performer and it was not until the era of Garrick and Mrs. Siddons that the style they had brought to perfection was seriously challenged and the suggestion could be made that equals of Betterton and Barry were at last to be seen. The most important thing to bear in mind about the company over the eight years during which Congreve wrote for it was that it was composed of highly experienced performers, some of whom had been working together since just after the reopening of the theatres in 1660. The average age of the principals at the first performance of *The Way of the World* was probably close to forty. Betterton played Valentine in *Love for Love* with great success at just under sixty. From mature actors one would expect subtlety, economy, superb timing, and great authority of presence. One would not look for dash, sprightliness, and effortless *joie de vivre*—these were the speciality of the new crop of young performers coming up at Smock Alley and Drury Lane and the new repertoire Farquhar, Cibber, and Vanbrugh were creating for them.

What of the talents of the individual actors and actresses? In 1694

[4] *The Critical Works of John Dennis*, ed. E. N. Hooker (Baltimore, 1939), I, 418.

[5] Letter of 28 February 1778 in *Mozart's Letters*, ed. Eric Blom (Harmondsworth, 1956), p. 87. The German phrase is 'wie ein gutgemachts Kleid'.

Southerne created the role of Isabella in *The Fatal Marriage* for Elizabeth
Barry—a play and a part that were to hold the stage for over 150 years.
His comments on her acting in the dedication, while not giving
us much specific information about her style, reveal a performer who
could exercise complete control over her audiences:

> I could not, if I would, conceal what I owe Mrs. *Barry*; and I
> should despair of ever being able to pay her, if I did not imagine
> that I have been a little accessary to the great Applause, that every
> body gives her, in saying she out-plays her self; if she does that,
> I think we may all agree never to expect, or desire any Actor
> to go beyond that Commendation; I made the Play for her
> part, and her part has made the Play for me: It was a helpless
> Infant in the Arms of the Father, but has grown under her Care;
> I gave it just motion enough to crawl into the World, but by
> her power, and spirit of playing, she has breath'd a soul into
> it, that may keep it alive.

To Southerne, Mrs. Barry's greatness lay in the emotional depth
of her acting, particularly her scenes of pathos. Charles Gildon reported
her as saying of her performance as Monimia in Otway's *The Orphan*
that she could never speak the phrase 'Ah! poor *Castalio*!' without
weeping.[6] Congreve saw her in a rather different light. Her parts
in his plays were Laetitia in *The Old Batchelour*, Lady Touchwood in
The Double Dealer, Mrs. Frail in *Love for Love*, Zara in *The Mourning
Bride*, and Mrs. Marwood in *The Way of the World*—unfaithful wives,
scheming mistresses, and, in the tragedy, a figure of violent, ungoverned
passion. It is significant that he never gave her a sympathetic role:
these were reserved for Anne Bracegirdle. (Anthony Aston
observes tartly that Mrs. Barry 'outshined Mrs. Bracegirdle in *The
Mourning Bride* altho Mr. Congreve designed Almeria for that favour'.)
Aston also mentions 'a Manner of drawing out her Words, which
became her' and that 'her face somewhat preceded her Action, as
the latter did her Words',[7] a statement whose implications could be
the key to a whole art of acting.

In view of Congreve's personal affection for Mrs. Bracegirdle
and the fact that she created the role of the heroine in each of his

---

[6] Charles Gildon, *The Life of Mr. Thomas Betterton* (London, 1710), p. 40.

[7] Anthony Aston, *A Brief Supplement to Colley Cibber, Esq; his Lives of the late
famous Actors and Actresses* (1748) in *An Apology for the Life of Mr. Colley Cibber*,
ed. Robert W. Lowe (London, 1889), II, 302–3.

plays, it would seem desirable to reproduce Colley Cibber's description of her in full:

> Mrs. *Bracegirdle* was now, but just blooming to her Maturity; her Reputation, as an Actress, gradually rising with that of her Person; never any Woman was in such general Favour of her Spectators, which, to the last Scene of her Dramatick Life, she maintain'd, by not being unguarded in her private Character. This Discretion contributed, not a little, to make her the *Cara*, the Darling of the Theatre: For it will be no extravagant thing to say, scarce an Audience saw her, that were less than half of them Lovers, without a suspected Favourite among them: And tho' she might be said to have been the Universal Passion, and under the highest Temptations; her Constancy in resisting them, serv'd but to increase the number of her Admirers: And this perhaps you will more easily believe, when I extend not my Encomiums on her Person, beyond a Sincerity that can be suspected; for she had no greater Claim to Beauty, than what the most desirable *Brunette* might pretend to. But her Youth, and lively Aspect, threw out such a Glow of Health, and Chearfulness, that, on the Stage, few Spectators that were not past it, could behold her without Desire. It was even a Fashion among the Gay, and Young, to have a Taste or *Tendre* for Mrs. *Bracegirdle*. She inspired the best Authors to write for her, and two of them, when they gave her a Lover, in a Play, seem'd palpably to plead their own Passions, and make their private Court to her, in fictitious Characters. In all the chief Parts she acted, the desirable was so predominant, that no Judge could be cold enough to consider, from what other particular Excellence she became delightful.[8]

One of the authors who made his court was of course Congreve. She was successively his Araminta, his Cynthia, his Angelica, his Almeria, and finally and supremely Millamant. Cibber's description suggests that the effect of her acting was softer and warmer than might appear simply from her lines. In the case of Millamant he was quite specific about this. In her performance 'all the Faults, Follies and Affectation of that agreeable Tyrant, were venially melted down into so many Charms, and Attractions of a conscious Beauty.'[9] The

[8] *An Apology for the Life of Colley Cibber*, ed. B. R. S. Fone (Ann Arbor, 1968), pp. 97–8.
[9] Ibid., p. 98.

account is interesting in that this type of role had previously been the speciality of Susannah Mountfort, the creator of Belinda in *The Old Batchelour* and Lady Froth in *The Double Dealer* and rapturously praised by Cibber for her performances as the twittering Melantha in Dryden's *Marriage à la Mode* and a country simpleton in Durfey's *The Bath* (this last role suggesting that Congreve may also have had her in mind for Miss Prue). It is almost certainly significant for the genesis of Millamant that at the division of the company in 1695 Mrs. Mountfort, after some wavering, chose to stay at Drury Lane and was thus no longer in the same company as Mrs. Bracegirdle. Naturally Mrs. Bracegirdle tried her hand at a few of Mrs. Mountfort's parts and naturally the effect of these parts was changed in the process. The notion of an affected coquette who was also a woman of sense with a capacity for genuine affection was therefore quite probably as much the discovery of the actress as of the dramatist, a perfect example of collaboration in the sense given to the word a little earlier.

Another actress who served Congreve well was Elinor Leigh. She was Lucy, Sylvia's maid, in *The Old Batchelour*, Lady Plyant in *The Double Dealer*, Prue's nurse in *Love for Love*, and reached the climax of her career in creating the role of Lady Wishfort in *The Way of the World*. Cibber praised her 'very droll way of dressing the pretty Foibles of superannuated Beauties' and remembered her as 'the languishing Lady *Wishfort*'.[10]

For Betterton, or perhaps it would be fairer to say *with* Betterton, Congreve created the characters of Heartwell, Maskwell, Osmyn, and Fainall. He was also, at sixty, an extremely successful Valentine, although it has been suggested that this was a consequence of the division of the companies and that he was originally intended for Sir Sampson. (On the other hand at seventy-four he was still capable of a Hamlet that 'by the prevalent power of proper Manner, Gesture, and Voice, appeared through the whole drama a youth of great expectation, vivacity, and enterprise'.)[11] The parts in *The Old Batchelour*, *The Double Dealer*, and *The Way of the World* are all subsidiary character roles, the leads going to the younger men, Powell, Williams, and Verbruggen. They are also, like the parts Congreve gave Mrs. Barry, essentially unsympathetic: an elderly curmudgeon and two outright villains. But when Betterton was on stage it was his play

[10] Ibid., p. 93.

[11] Richard Steele, *The Tatler* for 22 September 1709 in *The Tatler*, ed. G. A. Aitken (London, 1898), II, 163–4.

Bc

and in the first two cases it took its title from him. When in 1695 the young actors at Drury Lane announced a performance of *The Old Batchelour* 'in Imitation of the Original', there was no doubt for a moment as to who was to be imitated. [12]

One of the pleasures of reading widely in Restoration drama, especially the tragedies, is that one gradually begins to build a sense of what Betterton's delivery must have been like. Certain phrases, certain suggestions of cadence and intonation, keep repeating themselves in his parts. Cibber makes it clear that, like his successor, Barton Booth, he was above all a vocal actor:

> In the just Delivery of Poetical Numbers, particularly where the Sentiments are pathetick, it is scarce credible, upon how minute an Article of Sound depends their greatest Beauty or Inaffection. The Voice of a Singer is not more strictly ty'd to Time and Tune, than that of an Actor in Theatrical Elocution: The least Syllable too long, or too slightly dwelt upon, in a Period, depreciates it to nothing; which very Syllable, if rightly touch'd, shall, like the heightening Stroke of Light from a Master's Pencil, give Life and Spirit to the whole. I never heard a Line in Tragedy come from *Betterton*, wherein my Judgment, my Ear, and my Imagination, were not fully satisfy'd; which, since his Time, I cannot equally say of any one Actor whatsoever. . . . [13]

Anthony Aston, much franker in his comments, describes Betterton's voice as 'low and grumbling' yet concedes that 'he could tune it by an artful Climax, which enforc'd universal Attention even from the Fops and Orange-Girls'. [14] Aston also gives us what is probably the most detailed description of Betterton's physical appearance, describing him as corpulent, clumsily made, large-headed and 'a little Pock-fretten' yet as generating an aura that was 'serious, venerable, and majestic'. The picture is one of an actor who without much help from physical appearance had come to exercise an absolute authority of presence.

Reading such accounts helps one to realize why *The Mourning Bride*, which, viewed as literature, remains a beautifully finished but more than slightly absurd baroque curiosity, should have been Congreve's greatest single success in the theatre. Comic acting in Congreve's time was probably not all that different from what one might still

---

[12] See Cibber, ed. Fone, p. 114.   [13] Ibid., p. 66   [14] Aston, pp. 299–300.

see today in a traditionally conceived revival of one of the plays, and Shakespeare seems to have been acted with some attention to psychological realism; but the 'heroic play', the Restoration's own contribution to the tragic genre, was a grandiose spectacle which drew on the full resources of the theatre, and required a style of acting which would only be seen today, if at all, in opera. The action took place against tall scenes in deep perspective whose aim was to dignify and enlarge the human figure. The men actors were splendid in classical armour augmented by wigs and feathers; the women had long trains carried by pages. Gesture was elaborate and rigidly formalized. The performers copied their poses from paintings and statues and were copied in turn by painters and sculptors: a Londoner wanting a crash course in baroque stage gesture might do worse than make a tour of the tombs in Westminster Abbey. Lines were declaimed with every artifice of rhetoric. In scenes depicting the stronger passions the audience might expect their ears to be 'roundly rattled'; but tender passages could be given a song-like intonation, variously described as 'speaking to a tone' and 'whining love'. Acting was directed straight at the audience and at least one school seems to have held that the performer should always be visible full face. Dene Barnett, to whom I am indebted for several of these observations, has suggested in conversation that for a baroque actor even to give the illusion that he was speaking to another, it would have been necessary for him to withdraw several feet to the rear. It is even possible that dialogues in serious plays were conducted in a kind of see-saw motion with the speaker always upstage and the receiver forward, a pattern that looked remarkably right—possibly because it recalled eighteenth century dance movements—when tried in Barnett's production of a Rameau opera at the 1972 Adelaide festival. The degree of audience involvement in the Restoration theatre seems to have been a variable factor, but when an audience did become involved it was with a fervour and demonstrativeness which are rarely seen today except perhaps, again, at operas. Each sentence, each phrase even, was a unit of acting requiring its own precise mood, vocal tone and gesture, and the successful detail would bring enthusiastic applause. Mrs. Siddons, possibly a less electric actress than Mrs. Barry, but essaying many of the same roles and certainly within the same tradition, treated her performances as a series of 'turns' to be followed by applause and a moment of relaxation.[15] That Congreve had a similar technique

[15] Roger Manvell, *Sarah Siddons, Portrait of an Actress* (London, 1970), p. 102.

in mind when he wrote *The Mourning Bride* can be seen from almost any of the more impassioned speeches.

To appreciate the rationale behind this approach to acting it is necessary to understand the dramatic aims of the plays which gave birth to it. Philip Parsons has made the important point that Restoration tragedy, or Restoration melodrama as he prefers to call it, is historically speaking heavily under the influence of the Caroline court masque.[16] The aim of a masque is by definition to give sensuous life to abstract formulations. In the Caroline masques the formulations had usually been political, a celebration of the goodness and bounty of the king for whose pleasure and in whose court they were performed. The writers of Restoration tragedy were also fond of political themes, but their central interest was in what we might call 'moral allegories of the passions'. The stage, to use words which Gildon put in the mouth of Betterton, was seen as 'the Seat of Passion in its various kinds',[17] and acting was essentially a matter of representing these kinds in the forms in which they had been categorized by Descartes (*Les Passions de l'Âme*) and illustrated by Le Brun, whose drawings were studied as eagerly by actors as by artists.[18] The actor or actress would come forward and 'do' a passion in a short aria-like speech, then perhaps proceed to another congruent with the role, and even a third, after which it would be time for another performer whose part embraced a different complex of passions to take over. The greater actors attempted more difficult problems, transitions, for instance, from one passion to its opposite. (Love to rage was a favourite; the effect is one of wild paranoia.) Conflicts of irreconcilable passions were also popular and were regarded as representing the furthest reach of acting virtuosity. Then there might be 'duets' between characters whose passions were strongly contrasted—*The Mourning Bride* is particularly rich in these. There was of course little or no realism to such displays. They were judged by the audience for their 'justness' and 'propriety'—that is for the degree to which they approximated to the generalized analyses of the passions given by moral writers and philosophers—however, it is also clear that they were able to create the most intense theatrical excitement, and that it was not only the

[16] See his 'Restoration Tragedy as Total Theatre' in *Restoration Literature: Critical Approaches*, ed. Harold Love (London: Methuen, 1972), pp. 27–68; esp. p. 28.

[17] *The Life of Mr Thomas Betterton*, p. 40.

[18] See Parsons' valuable 'Restoration Melodrama and its Actors', *Komos* II (1969–70), 81–8, esp. n. 13, p. 88.

rants and rages which gave rise to this. Artificial and remote as such an approach to drama seems to us, it was something that in the hands of Betterton and Barry had enormous theatrical vitality. No doubt to see them as Osmyn and Zara with Mrs. Bracegirdle as Almeria, Jack Verbruggen, a 'natural' actor whose speciality was scenes of unbridled emotion (which we would no doubt find most unnatural), as Manuel and the most renowned of stage villains, Samuel Sandford, as Gonsalez, was to behold a miracle that we can not even guess at. But then it was written to be their play and not ours.

It remains to say something of Congreve's theatre and the audiences who supported it. Congreve's plays received their premieres either at the United Company's theatre at Drury Lane or the 1695 secession-ists' converted tennis-court in Portugal St, *The Old Batchelour* and *The Double Dealer* at the first, and the three later plays at the second. Restoration theatres were cramped, unheated, smelly buildings, lit by wax candles. They had no foyer, no box-office, no bar, no coffee-counter, no lavatories, though they did, when funds permitted, run to considerable amounts of scroll work and gilded ornament. The audience was dispersed between the pit, a ring of boxes surrounding the pit roughly at stage level, and two galleries above the boxes. By modern standards the theatres were not large. The pit at Drury Lane probably held only ten or a dozen rows of benches, the boxes and galleries perhaps three. Maximum capacity was not much over a thousand. Despite the fondness of the age for brilliant masque effects and perspective scenery it was still basically a speaker's theatre, most of the acting taking place on a modified Elizabethan thrust stage giving close rapport with the audience. Van Voris points out that the Restoration stage accommodated two quite different modes of presen-tation—one, 'grandiose and operatic' behind the proscenium, and the other, 'talky, intimate, familiar' upon the apron.[19] The invaluable Cibber has given us a first-hand account of what it felt like to act on the Drury Lane stage at the time Congreve was writing:

> But when the Actors were in Possession of that forwarder Space, to advance upon, the Voice was then more in the Centre of the House, so that the most distant Ear had scarce the least Doubt, or Difficulty in hearing what fell from the weakest Utterance: All Objects were thus drawn nearer to the Sense; every painted Scene was stronger; every Grand Scene and Dance more ex-tended; every rich, or fine-coloured Habit had a more lively

[19] W. H. Van Voris, *The Cultivated Stance* (Dublin, 1965), pp. 102–3.

Lustre: Nor was the minutest Motion of a Feature (properly changing with the Passion, or Humour it suited) ever lost, as they frequently must be in the Obscurity of too great a Distance: And how valuable in Advantage the Facility of hearing distinctly, is to every well-acted Scene, every common Spectator is a Judge. A Voice scarce rais'd above the Tone of a Whisper, either in Tenderness, Resignation, innocent Distress, or Jealousy, suppress'd, often have as much concern with the Heart, as the most clamorous Passions; and when on any of these Occasions, such affecting Speeches are plainly heard, or lost, how wide is the Difference, from the great or little Satisfaction received from them?[20]

What is described in this passage is the ideal acoustic not only for Congreve but for Shakespeare as well. Nevertheless, it must not be thought that such perfection as Wren's Drury Lane could be repeated at will. When Congreve joined with Vanbrugh in 1704 to build a new theatre in the Haymarket it proved to be an acoustic disaster in which scarcely a word could be distinctly heard.

What of Congreve's audiences? Who were they and where did they come from? Books on Restoration drama are rarely in doubt about this matter and tend to contain phrases such as these (all relatively recent):

Perhaps even now no writer would dare base a comedy on the central situation used in *The Country Wife*. Yet there was no protest, it seems, from the audience: the tiny Court clique and its dependents, who were the main patrons of the theatre . . .

* * *

The promotion of mistresses rather than of the drama was the chief preoccupation of those theatre-going gentlemen.

* * *

The public theatres were often poorly attended, and the main part of the audience consisted of courtiers, hangers-on and prostitutes.

* * *

The theatre set lived in a kind of sophisticated Hobbesian state of Nature, and a natural hostility of manner had become the order of the day.

[20] Cibber, pp. 225-6.

It has only recently been realized that these notions, along with Dr. Johnson's castigation of the Restoration theatres as 'temples of dissolute licentiousness' and Macaulay's of their audiences as 'the most deeply corrupted part of a corrupted society', are ultimately restatements of remarks made about the theatres by a number of eighteenth century clergymen and busybodies who had probably never set foot in them and which were regarded as absurdly misinformed by those who had. The truth of the matter is much more likely to be that expressed by Donald C. Mullin in *The Development of the Playhouse*:

> A common misconception about the early public theatre of box, pit, and gallery is that it was undemocratic in design and purpose. One has visions of the nobility elegantly isolated in plush boxes while the rabble rioted in the pit below. Such a theatre exists only in the minds of historical novelists. The court theatre was attended on a hierarchal basis, but the public theatre was established and operated in order to make money. Places were available at various prices and anyone could sit wherever his purse would allow. The divisions were economic, not social, and while in some instances these may be considered to be one and the same, the reverse was usually the case.[21]

Recent studies of the Restoration audience, though still very tentative, suggest that the most important groups in terms of numbers were not prostitutes and time-wasters (though both were certainly in evidence) but public servants, professional men, law students, country worthies wintering in town, and the wives, families and servants of these. The representation of the court and courtiers has probably been exaggerated even for the earlier years of Charles II, and was certainly much diminished by Congreve's time. The extent to which 'citizens', i.e. merchants and shopkeepers, supported the theatre is still a subject of debate; however, a reference to them in Congreve's prologue to George Powell's *A Very Good Wife* would suggest that they were quite a significant element:

> Now, you our City Friends, who hither come
> By three a Clock, to make sure Elbow-room:
> While Spouse, tuckt up, does in her Pattens trudge it

---

[12] Donald C. Mullin, *The Development of the Playhouse* (Berkeley and Los Angeles, 1970), p. 62.

With Hankerchief of prog, like Trull with Budget,
And here, by turns, you eat Plumb-Cake, and judge it.
Pray be you kind, let me your Grace importune,
Or else—I gad I'll tell you all your Fortune.

The tone of this is admittedly satiric, but the same treatment is given elsewhere in the poem to the beaux, the ladies, and the authors, all of whom were presumably welcome. On the whole it seems quite possible that the composition of Congreve's audience was not very different in social range and distribution from that of the private theatres of Shakespeare's time. It was certainly more representative of society as a whole than the membership of the Royal Society. Drury Lane and Lincoln's Inn Fields were not theatres of the people in the way the Elizabethan public theatres had been and certain important things were lost through this, but they were far from being the coterie haunts of edificatory legend. One should therefore be very careful about coming to conclusions about Congreve or other Restoration dramatists on the basis of second-hand assumptions about the kind of theatregoer for whom their plays were intended. A good deal of what passes for critical comment on Restoration comedy is in fact a covert appeal to the belief that it was created expressly for a 'courtly elite' or 'gallants' or whatever other chimerical notion the writer may have of the Restoration audience, and can not therefore be allowed any greater degree of intelligence or sensitivity than might be credited to such creatures. A related idea is that the plays were attended by the kinds of people who are portrayed in them. Both assumptions are, to say the least, highly dubious.

2

The Old Batchelour

I

Congreve appears to have drafted *The Old Batchelour* in 1689, shortly after his arrival in England, at a time when he had little or no contact with professional writers. In 1692 it was shown to Southerne, who brought it to Dryden. The aging ex-laureate was greatly taken with it, made some minor adjustments to the order of the scenes to give it 'the fashionable cutt of the town,'[1] and used his influence to have it acted. The first performance, on 9 March 1693, was the greatest personal triumph the London stage had seen since Otway's *Venice Preserv'd* eleven years earlier.

The twenty-three-year-old dramatist is hailed in the complimentary verses Southerne wrote for the first edition as the 'crown prince' of the Muses' land (Dryden being the king) and in the opening lines of the play Congreve delineates the boundaries of his dramatic realm with the peremptoriness appropriate to an heir-apparent. He begins with a dismissal of a number of things which are not, in what follows, to be taken into account—namely wisdom, 'business', knowledge and virtue. Wisdom and 'business' are dealt with first.

> *Bellmour. Vainlove,* and abroad so early! good Morrow; I
> thought a Contemplative Lover could no more have
> parted with his Bed in a Morning, than a' could have slept
> in't.
> *Vainlove. Bellmour,* good Morrow—Why truth on't is, these

[1] Southerne's notes on Congreve for the *General Dictionary* in *William Congreve: Letters and Documents,* ed. John C. Hodges (London, 1964), p. 151.

early Sallies are not usual to me; but Business as you see
Sir——— (*Shewing Letters.*) And Business must be follow'd,
or be lost.
Bellmour. Pox o' Business———And so must Time, my
Friend, be close pursued, or lost. Business is the rub of Life,
perverts our Aim, casts off the Bias, and leaves us wide and
short of the intended Mark.
Vainlove. Pleasure, I guess you mean.
Bellmour. Ay, what else has meaning?
Vainlove. Oh the Wise will tell you———
Bellmour. More than they believe———Or understand.
Vainlove. How how, *Ned,* a wise Man say more than he
understands?
Bellmour. Ay ay, pox Wisdom's nothing but a pretending to
know and believe more than really we do.

[I.i.1–20]

The next thing to go is learning, at least the academic kind; there is
more to be found, we discover, in the false spelling of a love-letter
Vainlove has dropped than in all Cicero. Following this, Congreve
turns his attention to virtue. Much as we are expected to accept without demur in *The Way of the World* that Mirabell is to be admired
for having married off his mistress on a false alarm of pregnancy to
a man whom he knows to be worthless, so here we must think no
less highly of Bellmour for having supplied Vainlove's place in the
dark with Sylivia; an action which by any legal definition constitutes
rape, and which is perpetrated upon a woman who, as Bellmour
himself is prepared to concede, is genuinely devoted to Vainlove.
Congreve seems almost to be daring us to make the obvious objections
and to take the consequence, which would be to reject not merely
Bellmour but the comedy in which Bellmour is presented to us as
a rational and likeable human being. (It should be noted right at the
start that Congreve's wits, both male and female, are by everyday
standards a pretty unpleasant lot, given to vicious social infighting,
brutal practical jokes, and when money or sex are in question outright standover tactics.) What is happening in these first speeches of
The Old Batchelour is very similar to what happens in the opening
lines of Marlowe's *Doctor Faustus* or in the speech to the gold at the
beginning of Jonson's *Volpone,* an item by item dismissal of received
values which the protagonists find irrelevant to their individual

situations. The difference is that in the earlier plays the lawful sciences rejected by Faustus and the human affections spurned by Volpone are ultimately to prove relevant after all and the characters who rejected them to stand condemned by them. In *The Old Batchelour* there is no such reversal. We are simply told to forget about these things until the play is over. And most of us are perfectly happy to do this.

Having resigned ourselves to the loss of wisdom and the rest we are offered in their place two other goals for endeavour, namely pleasure and wit, and once again are in a position where, if we are to accept the play, we have no alternative but to accept a facility in these as our touchstone for determining the relative worths of its characters.

> Come come, leave Business to Idlers, and Wis-
> dom to Fools; they have need of 'em: Wit, be my Faculty;
> and Pleasure, my Occupation; and let Father Time shake
> his Glass.
>
> [I.i.22–5]

It is Bellmour who advances these opinions; however, any appearance of division between him and Vainlove is wholly illusory, for the latter is so sublime an epicurean that even the modicum of wisdom and business contingent upon the consummation of an intrigue—the 'drudgery of loving' as Heartfree puts it for him—is an insupportable fatigue. Assent is all he seeks for, and then only when it is not too freely granted. Having received it without any serious preliminary petition on his own part from Mrs. Fondlewife and Sylvia, he is prepared to let Bellmour supply his place with both of them. And yet despite this last extremity of sexual connoisseurship, and despite Heartwell's brusque description of Vainlove as 'one of Love's April-fools', it is clear that insofar as there is a hierarchy of relative personal merit among the male characters he stands at the top of it, certainly higher than Bellmour. For of the two principles of action, wit and pleasure, it is the first which is to be valued most highly; in fact the witty man's initial choice of pleasure rather than business, wisdom, learning, or virtue as the primary aim of human activity is itself the consequence of the powers of right judgement conferred upon him by the possession of wit. Moreover, of the many varieties of pleasure available to him, it is those requiring the exercise of wit which he will

instinctively find most pleasing. There is ultimately more savour in
the perfection of a malicious stratagem or epigram with Vainlove
than in 'drudgery in the Mine' with Bellmour. Of course, wit is not
merely a matter of stratagems and epigrams—how much more we
will be considering shortly—neither is pleasure merely a matter of
prodigies of fornication. Even for Bellmour, a willing enough labourer
in the mine, the degree of pleasure experienced is dependent on the
degree of imagination exercised in its procurement— 'the deeper
the Sin the sweeter'. It is clearly important to him that the book he
bears with him when he enters Alderman Fondlewife's house disguised
as Tribulation Spintext should be the only proper and appropriate
book, Scarron's *The Innocent Adultery*: 'If I had gone a-Whoring
with the *Practice of Piety* in my Pocket,' he complains, 'I had never
been discover'd' [IV.iv.109-11]—but then the sin would have been
that much less deep. No doubt for a different woman there would
have been a different book. Sharper, another character for whom we
are instructed, slightly in spite of ourselves, to feel admiration, is
in search of money, not women, but even money is to be acquired
wittily, and the act of its acquisition from the impercipient to be
dignified as an exercise of wit in its own right. 'You . . . are bound,'
he tells Bellmour at the close of Act I 'For Love's Island: I, for the
Golden Coast./May each succeed in what he wishes most.' Each
course is equally worthy of enshrinement in epigram since each is
to centre on the exercise of wit. Wit is also the supreme palliative:
something wittily done can hardly be wrongly done. After hearing
Bellmour's fabricated account of the circumstances which have led
to his appearance in Vainlove's place at the assignation, Laetitia
concludes in an aside that 'either *Vainlove* is not guilty, or he has
handsomly excused him'. Clearly it does not matter much which
of the two alternatives is in fact the case. A handsome enough excusing
will atone for anything simply because it is handsome.

II

Wit, therefore, is the key value not only of the play's world but of
the play itself. In 1671, in the preface to *An Evening's Love or the Mock
Astrologer*, Dryden had attempted a critical justification of the comedy
of wit, using terms that point directly towards *The Old Batchelour*
and help explain his enthusiasm for it. To Dryden, ' . . . the business
of the poet is to make you laugh: when he writes humour, he makes

folly ridiculous; when wit, he moves you, if not always to laughter, yet to a pleasure that is more noble.'[2] It was in this 'nobler pleasure' that he saw the highest manifestation of comedy. It resided in wit, and more particularly in repartee, rapid, impromptu word-play involving more than one person. This was to be preferred even to the more judicious, reflective forms of wit that found expression in moral generalization:

> As for repartee in particular; as it is the very soul of conversation, so it is the greatest grace of comedy, where it is proper to the characters. There may be much of acuteness in a thing well said; but there is more in a quick reply. . . .[3]

This fascination with the quick reply will be seen over and over again in *The Old Batchelour*. Largely because of this, the scenes between Vainlove and Bellmour, and between these two and Belinda and Araminta, have much the effect of a tennis match. To say something is to challenge another person to supply an apposite retort. Hardly a statement can be let pass without an addition, a qualification, a reversal, an analogical prolongation, an illustration by way of simile, or a witty contradiction of some kind or another. In II.ii. Bellmour uses the image of buckets in a well to describe his relationship with Belinda: ' . . . my Tyrant there and I, are two Buckets that can never come together.' In a flash Belinda has seized on the image and turned it back against him: 'Nor are ever like—Yet we often meet and clash.' The onus is now on Bellmour to continue the rally. Sadly he can manage nothing better than a clumsy pun on the first part of her statement: 'How never like! marry *Hymen* forbid.' Unable to carry this particular line any further he serves up another metaphor which is sustained with alterations for no fewer than six speeches:

> *Bellmour.* But this it is to run so extravagantly in Debt; I have laid out such a world of Love in your Service, that you think you can never be able to pay me all: So shun me for the same reason that you would a Dun.

[2] John Dryden, Preface to *An Evening's Love: or the Mock Astrologer* (1671) in *Of Dramatic Poesy and other Critical Essays*, ed. George Watson (London, 1962), I, 152.
[3] Ibid., p. 149.

Belinda. Ay, on my Conscience, and the most impertinent and troublesome of Duns———A Dun for Mony will be quiet, when he sees his Debtor has not wherewithal——— But a Dun for Love is an eternal Torment that never rests———

Bellmour. Till he has created Love where there was none, and then gets it for his pains. For importunity in Love, like importunity at Court; first creates its own Interest, and then pursues it for the Favour.

Araminta. Favours that are got by Impudence and Importunity, are like Discoveries from the Rack, when the afflicted Person, for his ease, sometimes confesses Secrets his Heart knows nothing of.

Vainlove. I should rather think Favours, so gain'd, to be due Rewards to indefatigable Devotion———For as Love is a Deity, he must be serv'd by Prayer.

Belinda. O Gad, would you would all pray to Love then, and let us alone.

[II.ii.121–43]

The passage is a thoroughly characteristic example of Restoration repartee. Each statement seizes on an element from its predecessor, develops it in an unexpected way, and is itself developed by the next speaker. Like Dryden, Congreve seems to see the wit of repartee both as the highest kind of comic pleasure, and as the distinguishing badge of gentility. When his superior characters come together, this elaborate verbal tennis is the means by which they make their superiority manifest.

From the evidence provided by exchanges such as these we are able to attempt a preliminary definition of the protean faculty of wit and to identify an important respect in which Congreve's notion of its dramatic function is in advance of Dryden's. Dryden's discussion of wit presents it simply as a game with words, something which is essentially decorative. In Congreve, although the verbal surface may be brilliant, wit is never merely verbal. Behind the rapid retorts and dizzying shifts in rhetorical direction, there is always a sense of personalities in conflict. We may even come to feel that wit as practised by true adepts is fundamentally a way of interacting with others, only secondarily an art of verbal challenge and response; and that epigram and repartee are nothing more than single weapons from a large armoury whose function is to secure a position of dominance for the possessor in social relationships. This point will become clearer if we return to the passage just discussed directing our attention this time not to the flow of the exchanges, but to the interactions which are taking place in the course of that flow.

The passage begins with a simile of a kind very common in Restoration drama in which an action with pretensions to dignity is equated reductively with another action which is seen to be self-interested, mechanical or compulsive. The topics of this class of simile are limited: gamblers and thieves are called on as types of greed, lawyers and whores of dissimulation, poets of poverty, superannuated ladies of vanity, and parsons of sycophancy. In this case, the equivalence proposed is between Belinda's refusal to hear Bellmour's addresses and a debtor's attempt to evade a creditor:

> *Bellmour.* I have laid out such a
> world of Love in your Service, that you think you can
> never be able to pay me all: So shun me for the same
> reason that you would a Dun.

The passage is witty, not so much in its choice of simile, which is not particularly original, as in its rightness for the rhetorical situation. The explanation advanced for Belinda's behaviour is fantastical but is putting her in a position requiring defence. It involves the technique that D. R. M. Wilkinson calls 'imputing'.[4] Bellmour is challenging her to replace an interpretation of her behaviour flattering to him with another that will restore the balance in her direction, which, as an adept at the game, she does without hesitation:

> *Belinda.* Ay, on my Conscience, and the most impertinent and
> troublesome of Duns———A Dun for Mony will be
> quiet, when he sees his Debtor has not wherewithal———
> But a Dun for Love is an eternal Torment that never
> rests———

Belinda's choice of alternatives in framing her response to Bellmour was either to contradict his analogy with another or to accept the analogy but in a way which reversed its implications. The most effective tactic would probably have been to counter one analogy with another, thus forcing Bellmour into the position of having to coin a third. However, Bellmour's wit is not merely wit for wit's sake, it is wit being used to put him in a favourable position for pressing

[4] D. R. M. Wilkinson, *The Comedy of Habit* (Leiden, 1964), pp. 106–7.

his arguments of love upon Belinda. He has, even if frivolously, made a public declaration that he is in love with her (which may be true, although his statements at I.i.165–75 give reason for doubt). This requires a defensive movement on her part. Her reaction is therefore to acknowledge his analogy and in doing so to acknowledge the declaration of love, but in a way which, by turning the declaration to ridicule, implies an outright rejection of his proposal. Her measure is essentially protective—in Wilkinson's terminology, a 'disclaimer'.[5] Its aim is to deny him any minor advantage that might encourage more aggressive measures. He is 'an eternal Torment that never rests' which, decoded, is as close as she can come within the rules of the wit game to outright rudeness.

But Bellmour is now ready to respond in kind. Seizing on her restatement of the analogy before she has had time to complete it, he tacks on another term. If he is a torment, he is a torment who never rests

> Till he has created Love where there was none, and then gets it for his pains. For importunity in Love, like importunity at Court; first creates its own Interest, and then pursues it for the Favour.

To be a dun in love, even a tormenting, unresting dun, is not so foolish a policy after all because it will eventually produce love in return. Here Bellmour, having failed to get Belinda to say she loves him, is challenging her to say specifically she will never love him. In support of his rather curious claim he again appeals to an analogy from an area of human behaviour whose self-interested character is indisputable: He will triumph in the way an importunate suitor at Court triumphs—by sheer, dogged persistence. However, Araminta has spotted the flaw in his logic and usurps Belinda's right of reply to draw very different implications from Bellmour's analogy, which was admittedly a rather desperate one:

> *Araminta.* Favours that are got by Impudence and Importunity, are like Discoveries from the Rack, when the afflicted Person, for his ease, sometimes confesses Secrets his Heart knows nothing of.

[5] Ibid., pp. 105–6.

This is in a sense a double reprimand to Bellmour. His strategy has been to create a rhetorical opening that would require Belinda to accept or deny the proposal from his side that she is, or must infallibly become, in love with him. Araminta, as she neatly develops his analogy, is at the same time using it to resolve the pattern of imputation followed by disclaimer which has emerged during the encounter and which without her intervention might have lasted as long as Belinda and Bellmour had wit and breath. Even if Bellmour's importunity were to extort an assurance of love from Belinda, it need not represent her real thoughts; indeed, insofar as he has been arguing from a parallelism between the motives of lovers and those of the self-interested world of duns and politicians, it could never do so. The missile has been turned back towards its point of origin.

At this point Vainlove enters the duel and the game which has been played by Bellmour and Belinda is suddenly passed over to himself and Araminta. Vainlove's contribution gives an appearance of being a logical development of the preceding argument, although it is in fact a fresh statement of the theme of the persistent lover and the unresponsive mistress with which the exchange began. His aim is, like Bellmour's, to extract an acknowledgement of his role as professed lover from the women:

> *Vainlove.* I should rather think Favours, so gain'd, to be due Rewards to indefatigable Devotion———For as Love is a Deity, he must be serv'd by Prayer.

The analogy is conventional enough but has the advantage that where Bellmour has been scaling down courtship to the level of business and politics, Vainlove is now elevating it to that of religious devotion. Belinda, as in her recounter upon Bellmour a moment earlier, tries shock tactics to put him in his place—an expression of outright rejection:

> *Belinda.* O Gad, would you would all pray to Love then, and let us alone.

But Vainlove is her equal here, and in what is probably the most elegant of the exchanges deftly transmutes her suggestion that the men should pray to love into a command to make love: 'You are the Temples of Love, and 'tis through you, our Devotion must be convey'd.'

Cc

Having reached this point the contest is close to being won. The aim of it has been to lure the women into an acceptance of a verbal formula that will imply a recognition, even if only in jest, of the men's role as lovers. The game on the women's part is to avoid this, or as a second-best to force the men into accepting a verbal formula acknowledging rejection. If we can see the whole thing as a speeded-up version of the kind of semantic manipulation that might take hours, months, or years at a truce-table or international conference we are probably closest to understanding its real nature. Of course, as with the communiqués of international conferences, the players are well aware that the verbal formulation does not necessarily represent reality. And yet these formulations are of importance insofar as they give the parties a chance to act as if they did, in their jockeying for further initiatives.

For the men have one trick up their sleeves that the women cannot use: having gained the right kind of rhetorical advantage they can then suddenly become 'serious', either by a shift into formal courtship in the grand manner, full of 'flames' and high-flown protestations of passion, or else by drawing direct attention to the sexual implications of the game, the fact that the real thing at issue is not whether one player is to succeed in outfoxing the other in wit, but whether or not the relationship is to take them as far as bed and, if so, on what terms. In his image of the women as 'Temples of Love' and the ambiguity of the 'Devotion' offered, Vainlove is nicely poised to move in either of these directions—full-blown romantic rhetoric or *double entendre*. If his choice were the first of these, he would lapse, having first placed his hand on his heart and inclined his head languidly to one side, into the conventional whining tone of the Restoration stage lover, as burlesqued by Careless in IV.i. of *The Double Dealer*. The second possibility would be that taken up later in the scene by Bellmour with his 'villainous Signs' and 'standing Argument'. The only reaction open to the women is therefore to break off the wit encounter before the seriousness can go too far. But first of all Vainlove has to be very firmly put in his place by the one piece of information that will inevitably deflate the intoning male—that such assurances are by no means reserved for Araminta and Belinda. Luckily the temple image has permitted an acceptably witty transition to this idea:

> *Araminta.* Rather poor silly Idols of your own making, which,
> upon the least displeasure you forsake, and set up new

—Every Man, now, changes his Mistress and his
Religion, as his Humour varies or his Interest.
[II.ii.146–9]

Vainlove seems to have an answer to this too: it is interesting to
speculate what it might have been. But he is given no chance to
deliver it. Feeling, no doubt, that the men are having too much of a
good thing, and that Belinda, who is really something of a scatter-
brain, is not the most reliable of allies, Araminta brings the exchange
to a close with an explicit 'Nay come, I find we are growing serious . . .'
—by which she means that the game of wit is on the point of leading
to something more unsettling.

Looking back on this passage, it will be seen that the linguistic
features of the repartee are not of any great complexity. Its art resides
in the ability to embody arguments in analogies and to contradict an
opponent's points by reapplying, extending, or replacing his analogies.
Slowed down for inspection it turns out to be fairly predictable, even
formulaic. Against this we should realize that the real dramatic
interest of the passage just analysed is not the polish and ingenuity
of the analogical fencing, agreeable as this may be at a fairly superficial level, but the sense behind this of subtle shifts in the relationship
of the fencers. Of course these things are not nearly so evident on a
first seeing or reading as they become after analysis, and it is necessary
to stress that the exchange which has taken several pages to discuss
would occupy less than a minute's playing time, equally that the mood
of the scene is basically one of light-hearted exhilaration. And yet
even on a first encounter we would be prepared, I think, to acknowledge that this is an exchange between realized characters, not just
elegant cut-outs, and that the contest is for much higher stakes than
the pleasure of winning. It is possible that the witty lovers have found
partners with whom marriage could be a meaningful or at least a
tolerable relationship. It is equally possible, and, given what we
have seen of the men elsewhere, not implausible, that the light-
hearted rhetoric of the wit game masks a heartless readiness to exploit
others or a neurotic urge to dominate in all relationships. The basic
posture of the game is defensive: it is important to give nothing away—
even in jest. One is aware of an element of anxiety in the game—to
fail at it would be a source of pain in itself, but might also leave the
loser vulnerable to a predatory lover or mistress. And how much
security is there even in friendship? The introductory scene between

Araminta and Belinda before the arrival of the men, shows that they too have their mutual reservations and defences. Belinda can no more reveal her feelings for Bellmour to Araminta than she could to Bellmour himself, while Araminta is no less industrious than he in trying to force an acknowledgement. The surface exuberance muffles but by no means negates the serious implications of the material. The comedy of wit is only a few steps removed from the comedy—if it is indeed comedy—of isolation.

III

I have been trying in the previous few pages to show that wit for Congreve's heroes and heroines is not simply a verbal skill but a mode of personal interaction, and that because of this it is possible to claim that Congreve's wit is more intrinsically dramatic than is allowed for in Dryden's theorizing, or for that matter in the older dramatist's own practice. Dryden sees wit as theatrical, it is true, but theatrical in a way which isolates it from the other elements of a play. Repartee and the conversation of gentlemen are to be relished for their own sake independently of their place in the dramatic whole. Congreve differs in regarding the wit of his characters as a set of clues to personality and social capacity. This means that it is never enough to stop at the verbal surface: the real interest of the dramatist is not in wit considered in itself but in what is adumbrated through the medium of wit.

A second wit exchange which has already been quoted extensively is that between Vainlove and Bellmour at the very beginning of the play, the exchange which so perfectly and economically establishes the tone and moral *données* of what is to follow. What we may not notice, so effortlessly is it done, is that the exchange has also shown the two as characters perhaps as fully as they are to be shown, and established an opposition between them that is to hold good for the entire play. On one hand we have the volatile Bellmour with his extravagant conceits and rhodomontades, on the other the sardonic and, for a wit, rather unloquacious Vainlove. The contrasting styles of their wit reveal an element of dramatic conflict. If it is Bellmour who gets most of the running in the initial exchange, it is also Bellmour who has to do most of the work—the drudgery of analogizing. The very fact that Vainlove does not feel obliged to enter into competition with Bellmour suggests that he is confident of his own superiority, an interpretation which is reinforced by the physical suggestiveness of his initial gesture in throwing the letters down, and Bellmour's stooping to pick them up. Similarly, that Bellmour is putting on such a dazzling display suggests that he acknowledges Vainlove's superior status and is anxious for his approbation. The relationship of the two in the wit exchange is thus of the same kind as in their sexual predations. Exactly as Vainlove gets Bellmour to take care of his unsolicited lovemaking for him, he is also content for him in the first few minutes of the scene to look much more like a wit than he does himself. But when Vainlove does begin to show his paces, we sense the assurance, and the superiority, at once; his character of Fondlewife has a weight, a conciseness, and a psychological penetration which make Bellmour seem florid and diffuse:

> A kind of Mungril Zealot, sometimes very precise and peevish: But I have seen him pleasant enough in his way; much addicted to Jealousie, but more to Fondness: So that as he is often Jealous without a Cause, he's as often satisfied without Reason.
>
> [I.i.106–10]

A similar kind of placing emerges from the conversation of Araminta and Belinda before the entry of the men in II.ii. In each case the tendency is to place the showier and more loquacious of the wits—the 'extravagant' in R. J. Jordan's term[6]—on a lower rung than the terser and more guarded.

Whether or not such conflicts are regarded as part of the 'action' of the play is largely a matter of how we define that problematical word.[7] They do not, in the cases mentioned, extend to the level of plot; but I would suggest that they are certainly one of the main dramatic interests the play has to offer, and insofar as the aim and end of its action, as the term is conventionally conceived, is to establish a ranking among the characters on the basis of their capacities for survival in a testing and combative world—a contention for which the comedy's concluding scene will, I hope, be regarded as sufficient evidence—these conflicts of personal style are at least as important to the drama as those which give rise to the various intrigues. A conflict which does eventually erupt at the plot level is that between

[6] In his 'The Extravagant Rake in Restoration Comedy' in *Restoration Literature: Critical Approaches*, ed. Harold Love (London: Methuen, 1972), pp. 69–90.

[7] For a characteristically wide-ranging account of the issues involved see Harold Brooks's 'The Name of Action', *Komos* II (1969–70), 37–49.

Vainlove and Bellmour on one side and Heartwell on the other;
but the elements of this conflict are clearly stated through the wit
long before they become manifest in action. In I.i. Bellmour engages
in an extended wit exchange with Heartwell. On the face of it the
two appear evenly matched, at least in the primary business of keeping
the returns in the air. One may even feel that in this particular match
Heartwell has the better of things. On the other hand, we will become
aware, if we are attentive, of certain features of Heartwell's manage-
ment of the wit game which are prognostic of his subsequent defeat.

The analogical wit of *The Old Batchelour* has two basic components.
The first is rhetorical agility and inventiveness, the power of manu-
facturing replies which while being elegant and unexpected also put
difficulties in the way of the responder. This is the faculty which
Congreve's contemporaries would probably have distinguished as
'fancy'. The second component is what Dryden in one of the several
senses he gave the word called 'judgement' but we would probably
call experience—that is, the possession of a store of images of human
life, especially those of a reductive tendency, on which to draw for
one's analogies. Even a cursory examination of the first exchange
will show that Bellmour's wit is stronger in the first faculty and that
Heartwell places more reliance on the latter. The difference is clear
right from Bellmour's first, leisurely greeting:

> How now *George*, where hast thou been snarling odious
> Truths, and entertaining company like a Physician, with
> discourse of their diseases and infirmities? What fine Lady
> hast thou been putting out of conceit with her self, and
> perswading that the Face she had been making all the
> morning was none of her own? for I know thou art as
> unmannerly and as unwelcome to a Woman, as a Look-
> ing glass after the Small-pox.
>
> [I.i.180–7]

To make a slight qualification to the distinction just drawn, Bellmour
is certainly taking images from experience here, but it is not the
substance of the images that catches our attention so much as the
grace and ingenuity with which the ideas are put. The images please
through an effortless elegance which is the reverse of Heartwell's
brusque, ungracious, but at the same time forceful particularizing:

> I confess I have not been sneering fulsome Lies and
> nauseous Flattery, fawning upon a little tawdry Whore,

that will fawn upon me again, and entertain any Puppy
that comes; like a Tumbler with the same tricks over and
over. For such I guess may have been your late employ-
ment.

[I.i.188–93]

Heartwell is replying to Bellmour in kind as the game requires,
but his images have a physical solidity which Bellmour's lack. Our
attention is seized by the subject, rather than the style.

The distinctions are perhaps at this stage rather fine ones but they
grow broader as the exchange continues. Heartwell speaks of Vainlove
using the (rather mundane) image of a ship that never comes to har-
bour. Sharper seizes on this gleefully but without adding anything
really sparkling to the invention:

That's because he always sets out in foul Weather,
loves to buffet with the Winds, meet the Tide and sail in
the Teeth of opposition.

[I.i.201–3]

Heartwell's reply to this keeps up the analogy but again in a terse,
prosaic way: 'What has he not drop't Anchor at *Araminta*?' There is
no new leap of the imagination here, merely a much-exercised reflex.
However, it is just at this point that Bellmour steps in and snatches
victory in the exchange with an image of real originality and distinction, which is also perhaps the most penetrating single thing said in
the play about Vainlove:

Truth on't is she fits his temper best, is a kind of
floating Island; sometimes seems in reach, then vanishes
and keeps him busied in the search.

[I.i.205–7]

This sort of thing is clearly beyond Heartwell. Where he succeeds
in the debate is by the sheer trenchancy of his denunciations of the
younger men and an almost Juvenalian ability to suggest that the
things he refers to are directly present to his eyes and ears and nose.
Consider him, for instance, on the subject of Vainlove:

I am for having every body be what they pretend
to be; a Whoremaster be a Whoremaster; and not like

Vainlove, kiss a Lap-Dog with passion, when it would disgust him from the Lady's own Lips.

[I.i.253–6

on the wits as a group:

> I confess you that are Women's Asses bear greater burdens, are forced to undergo Dressing, Dancing, Singing, Sighing, Whining, Rhyming, Flattering, Lying, Grinning, Cringing, and the drudgery of loving to boot.

[I.i.272–5]

on love after excessive courtship:

> Ay, why to come to Love through all these incumbrances is like coming to an Estate overcharg'd with Debts, which by the time you have pay'd, yields no further profit than what the bare tillage and manuring of the Land will produce at the expense of your own Sweat.

[I.i.277–81]

It will be noted that only the last of the three passages quoted is in fact an analogy. More commonly Heartwell's wit is simply illustrative mimicry—as in his superb imitation of a cuckold husband (one of a number of suggestions of Wycherley's Pinchwife and Manly in the character):

> *Heartwell.* Ay there you've nick't it—there's the Devil upon Devil—Oh the Pride and Joy of Heart 'twould be to me, to have my Son and heir resemble such a Duke—to have a fleering Coxcomb scoff and cry, Mr. your Son's mighty like his Grace, has just his smile and air of's Face. Then replies another—methink he has more of the Marquess of such a place, about his Nose and Eyes; though a' has my Lord what d'ee-cals Mouth to a Tittle—Then I to put it off as unconcern'd, come chuck the Infant under the chin, force a smile and cry, ay, the Boy takes after his Mothers relations—when the Devil and she knows, 'tis a little Compound of the whole Body of Nobility.

[I.i.317–28]

When Heartwell does use analogical wit, it tends to involve shorter mental jumps than is usual in the wit of Bellmour and Vainlove.

In fact he does not generally use analogy as a means to heighten our sense of the nature of an action, but rather as a device for intensifying feeling by bringing together a number of related particulars inspiring the same kind of contempt or revulsion as the thing with which they are compared. Such wit is a devastating weapon in argument but gives no sense of the lightning-swift responsiveness to new challenges which is the most consistent feature of the younger men's wit. The 'experience' on which Heartwell's wit relies is something fixed and stable, not a general theory of motivations, but a collection of solid sights and sounds. As a result, when he is confronted with a new and unexpected situation wit fails him completely. He is deceived by the simulated innocence of Sylvia; he finds himself unable to command his emotions even when (as his agonized asides show) he is fully aware of the peril of his predicament; finally, in the confrontation with Belinda at the close of the play, he loses control even of behaviour and descends to pure railing:

> ...How have I deserv'd this of you? Any of ye? Sir, have I
> impair'd the Honour of your House, promis'd your
> Sister Marriage, and whor'd her? Wherein have I injured
> you? Did I bring a Physician to your Father when he lay
> expiring, and endeavour to prolong his life, and you
> One-and-twenty? Madam, have I had an Opportunity
> with you and bauk'd it? Did you ever offer me the Favour
> that I refus'd it?
>
> [V.ii.50–8]

The repeated dagger-thrusts are ferociously effective but at the same time signalize a total breakdown in the wit's ability to govern the course of face-to-face encounters. The narrow range of Heartwell's wit which gives him solidity and force as a character, also makes him inflexible and unable to adapt. His verbal incapacities are thus a faithful index of his social incapacities. Deeper than either lies an even more serious limitation: he is unable to deal effectively with anything he has not tried and tested in the past.

The contrast between Heartwell and the true wits allows us to gain a deeper understanding of them as well as of him. We have considered wit as wordplay, as skill in the manipulation of social encounters, and as an element in the conduct of elaborate schemes of deceit. The ability to pluck exactly the right form of words out of the air without apparent effort is one aspect of it; the ability to seize a position of dominance in a face to face encounter is another; the quickwittedness of Sharper in his gulling of Sir Joseph and of Bellmour in extracting himself from his misfortune with the Fondlewifes is a third. But the basic skill of Congreve's wits is that of maintaining a continued openness to the unpredictable demands of a Heraclitean environment. Despite their fondness for generalizing about motivations, Bellmour and Vainlove know very well that they can never step into the same river twice. Those who, like Heartwell, think they can do this find it is not the same river after all, and are helplessly swept away.

<h2 style="text-align:center">IV</h2>

What I have had to say about *The Old Batchelour* will, I hope, have made clear that it is something more than a youthful *jeu d'esprit* composed of roughly equal quantities of farce and verbal fireworks. To go to the other extreme and endue it with a seriousness of purpose commensurate with the issues raised by its materials would be ridiculous, but it is not a distortion to say that it presents us with a consistently realized world, and that it has meaningful, if sometimes distasteful, answers to give to the problem of how the individual is to live in this world successfully (in the sense that a species perfectly adapted to its environment can be called 'successful'). Congreve's attitude remains fundamentally unserious, and I suppose we have to say shallow, in that he will not allow himself to be disturbed by the selfishness and lack of charity which are the basic facts of behaviour in this world and fails to see any incongruity in presenting these things in a spirit of near-total lightheartedness. Nevertheless, what he brings forward for our inspection has been seen honestly and clearly. When Sharper describes Vainlove's attributes as a lover as consisting of 'very little Passion, very good Understanding, and very ill Nature' [I.i.214–15] the implication is that this, if not a perfect, is at least a very sensible way of guarding oneself against the fates which befall the Heartwells of the world—and that Vainlove is on the whole to be admired for it. A justification along similar lines could easily be found for Lucy's principle enunciated in III.i.:

> Man, was by Nature Womans Cully made:
> We, never are but by our selves betray'd.
> [ll. 56–7]

The unspoken premise in each case is that given the world as the world is, only an impractical idealist would hope for anything better. If we are to get on with the business of living in this world, it has to be either on the wits' terms or on Sir Joseph's and Fondlewife's, and of these the former are surely preferable.

Having accepted this premise, it is then possible, and indeed necessary, to grade the characters according to the degree of aptitude which they show for the task. Like most of the better Restoration comedies, *The Old Batchelour* has as its central concern the measuring of its characters against a social ideal, an ideal which for want of a better term we might call 'gentility'. The term is one which is usually found today in the company of the adjective 'shabby' but in its original sense it is simply the abstract state of being a gentleman, and a gentleman, in Congreve's sense of the word, is a *town* gentleman, an *honnête homme*, someone who in addition to fortune and status possesses an unaffected polish, an unforced wit, and an infallible sense of style—the sort of person who might be expected to admire, or to write, a comedy such as *The Old Batchelour*. It is also, as we have seen, part of the equation that he and his female counterpart would be essentially selfish, at least where the interests of those outside the sanctified circle were concerned, and fairly well-insulated against the operations of natural sympathy. Finally, and preëminently, he must be a success —the criterion of success being what Henry James calls the 'aristocratic situation', namely 'to be in a better position for appreciating people than they are for appreciating you'[8]—with the difference that 'using' should in this context be added to 'appreciating'. With this ideal to guide us we are able to draw quite sharp distinctions between the differing levels of social accomplishment displayed in the comedy.

I have already given reasons to suggest that Vainlove should be put above Bellmour in any scale of success and I think it is also clear that Belinda should be ranked below Bellmour—at any rate he certainly has the edge on her in wit games and concludes by catching her in marriage pretty much on his own terms. I think it is also clear, however, that we are meant to put Araminta ahead of Vainlove. It is not merely that Vainlove is a highly unpleasant character, totally lacking in warmth, and Araminta a rather agreeable one—these matters do not affect the issue of who comes higher on the scale—it is rather Araminta's deft handling of the four-part wit game in II.ii, her rapid recovery from an unexpected and imperceptive rebuff from

8 *The Portrait of a Lady*, Chap. XIX.

Vainlove in IV.iii, and the neat chopping motion at the end with which she turns down his proposal of marriage. Indeed one hopes she will have the good sense to choose elsewhere.

The remaining figure of wit is Sharper. He is admittedly a rather peripheral character as far as the main intrigue goes and it is possibly a labour of superrogation to attempt to rank him. I would see him as coming below Bellmour but before Belinda; indeed the point of making such a placing is to show how ambiguous the position of Belinda is. Congreve's own comment on her is relevant here, made some years later when he was defending his portrayal, along with that of Prue in *Love for Love*, against the criticisms of Jeremy Collier:

> I only refer those two characters to the Judgment of any impartial Reader, to determine whether they are represented so as to engage any Spectator to imitate the Impudence of one, or the Affectation of the other; and whether they are not both ridiculed rather than recommended.[9]

This is not quite the effect a modern reader gets in either case, but there are certainly moments when Belinda comes perilously close to being ridiculous. She is diminished not only by her affectation and general lack of self-command, mercilessly dissected by Bellmour before we have even seen her and verified before our eyes by her first scene with Araminta, but even more tellingly by her miscalculation in the final taunting of Heartwell which infuriates him to the point of drawing his sword on her. It is hard to gauge what weight to give to her admission that she had 'touch'd a gall'd-beast till he winch'd'. At one level it suggests that she understands, and presumably forgives, Heartwell's desperation, an understanding which if we could credit it would cut across the callous complacency of the rest of the scene. But I doubt whether it indicates any real measure of sympathy: one would first, after all, have to assume she had fellow-feeling with galled beasts, which is not at all certain. The line could equally well be an additional sneer at Heartwell for having allowed himself to be reduced to the status of a beast, galled or otherwise. This would seem at least to be the implication of Vainlove's warning in the next line: '*Bellmour*, Give it over; you vex him too much; 'tis all serious to him.' Moreover when Heartwell finally makes a direct

---

[9] *Amendments of Mr. Collier's False and Imperfect Citations* (1698) in *The Mourning Bride, Poems and Miscellanies*, ed. Bonamy Dobrée (Oxford, 1928), p. 411.

reflection on Belinda's virtue, the others seem to feel she has deserved it, Vainlove maliciously returning her own image: 'Nay, tis a Sore of your own scratching . . .' The suggestion is that Belinda is not that far above Heartwell in the scale as she likes to think.

Moving down from Heartwell, who may be seen as a kind of amphibian, half in the world of the exploiters and half in that of the exploited, we come to the second level of predatory characters and, beyond them, the fools. Two of the former, Sylvia and Mrs Fondlewife, are certainly Heartwell's superiors in cunning. Sylvia deceives him entirely and should perhaps be placed above him in the hierarchy of wit were it not for her defencelessness before Vainlove and Bellmour and a suspicion that Heartwell's overthrow was in an indefinable way of his own making. Of the final group, the fools or out-and-out gulls, some preëminence must be given to the hulking but hollow Bluffe, who at least has the wit to outfox and manipulate Sir Joseph. This leaves the competition for bottom place to be decided between Sir Joseph and Fondlewife. Once again it is likely that an exact ranking is neither necessary nor possible, however, if one is to be made perhaps it should be in Sir Joseph's favour. He is at least aware that there is such a thing as wit and will occasionally, when he can forget about the weather, make hamfisted attempts at it. Fondlewife, on the other hand, is content at all times to remain what nature has made him—an alderman.

At the end of the play there are marriages, real and deceptive, intended and involuntary. The wits are rewarded, the errant chastised, the fools pillaged, the supernumerary mistresses preserved from shame in the one case and put in a good way of thriving in the other. Considered overall, the plot is slight, formulaic, and not particularly well integrated, and even among Congreve's contemporaries there were those who complained that the incidents were 'old and stale'.[10] Yet his primary concern, I have suggested, is not to present us with a satisfyingly unified narrative but to show us on which rung of the great ladder of the town each of his characters stands. The real 'action' is not the outward succession of events but the process of scrutiny and evaluation which attends them. Similarly, the concluding tableau is to be seen not as an image of comic renewal, but as a giving of emblematic form to a series of rankings which have been implicit in the play's material since the moment it began. Another way of

[10] Quoted by Davis (p. 27) from the Preface to Henry Higden's *Sir Noisy Parrott, or The Wary Widdow* (1693).

putting this is to say that *The Old Batchelour* is as much a masque as it is a comedy, something that we will see is also true of its successor.

My discussion of Congreve's first play has been chiefly concerned with those aspects which do most to illuminate his subsequent achievement and as a consequence of this I have had little to say about what are undoubtedly its greatest theatrical delights, the Sylvia, Wittol, and Fondlewife scenes. It is therefore possible that I have made it seem a darker and a more thoughtful play than we would ever want it to be in the theatre, though this is a misconception that could hardly survive even a brief return visit to the original. Congreve shows us a number of disturbing things, but will not allow us to become disturbed about them; indeed the peculiar discipline of the play, to return to a point raised at the beginning of the chapter, is its insistence that we adopt a lighthearted attitude towards matters which outside the theatre would make us anything but lighthearted. But even as he does this, Congreve knows, and we know, that sooner or later such things will have to be taken seriously, and in *The Double Dealer* we will see him making a determined effort—perhaps too determined —to atone for his earlier frivolity.

3

The Double Dealer

I

In December 1693, Dryden sent his friend William Walsh news of Congreve's second comedy, which had reached the stage in the previous month:

> His Double Dealer is much censured by the greater part of the Town: and is defended onely by the best Judges, who, you know, are commonly the fewest. Yet it gets ground daily, and has already been acted Eight times. The women thinke he has exposd their Bitchery too much and the Gentlemen are offended with him; for the discovery of their follyes: & the way of their Intrigues, under the notion of Friendship to their Ladyes Husbands. My verses, which you will find before it, were written before the play was acted, but I neither altered them nor do I alter my opinion of the play. [1]

The verses are the lines 'To my Dear Friend Mr. Congreve, on his Comedy, call'd The Double Dealer', a generous and moving tribute from the aging master to his brilliant protégé whom he saw as uniting the separate excellences of each of the previous masters of English comedy:

> In easie Dialogue is *Fletcher*'s Praise:
> He mov'd the mind, but had not power to raise.

---

[1] *The Letters of John Dryden*, ed. Charles E. Ward (Durham, U.S.A., 1942), p. 63.

> Great *Johnson* did by strength of Judgment please:
> Yet doubling *Fletcher*'s Force, he wants his Ease.
> In differing Tallents both adorn'd their Age;
> One for the Study, t'other for the Stage.
> But both to *Congreve* justly shall submit,
> One match'd in Judgment, both o'er-match'd in Wit.
> In Him all Beauties of this Age we see;
> *Etherege* his Courtship, *Southern*'s Purity;
> The Satire, Wit, and Strength of Manly *Witcherly*.
> [ll. 20–30]

The poem is also a proclamation of Congreve's right of succession
to Dryden in the laureateship—the laureateship of merit, that is, the
office itself having passed for political reasons to the Whig Thomas
Shadwell. Regrettably Dryden's enthusiasm for the play was not
shared by the public and it was to be some time before it could claim
the status of a stock comedy. Nevertheless, Congreve's circle of
friends seem to have been pleased with it, and one of them, William
Dove, contributed lines to the *Gentleman's Journal* which suggest
that they valued the play for much the same reasons they had its
predecessor—its gentlemanly ease and the brilliance and effortless
abundance of its verbal wit:

> Since Inspiration's ceas'd, I fain would know
> To whom thy wondrous store of Wit we owe?
> 'Tis more than e'er Philosophy could teach,
> How Imperfection should Perfection reach;
> Yet while thy Works with native Glory shine,
> And sprightly Phrazes render them divine,
> We think thou'rt sprung from the Prophetic Line.

The lines are obviously meant to embody the qualities they praise:
with their self-conscious straining after 'sprightly Phrazes' they might
easily have sprouted from the pen of some versifying Bellmour.

But *The Double Dealer*, as even a first reading will show, is far
from being a re-run of *The Old Batchelour*, and when Congreve came
to its defence against those who had failed to appreciate it in performance it was through a proclamation of artistic priorities very different from those implied by Dove's lines. In his lengthy dedication,
there is no reference at all to verbal wit. Instead we find Congreve
laying stress on the virtues of his comedy as an artifact, on his observance of the unities of time, place, and action, on the plausibility of

motive and characterization, and, more generally, on the virtues of the comedy as a well-made play according to the canons of neo-classical criticism.

> I design'd the Moral first, and to that Moral I invented the Fable, and do not know that I have borrow'd one hint of it any where. I made the Plot as strong as I could, because it was single, and I made it single, because I would avoid confusion and was resolved to preserve the three Unities of the Drama, which I have visibly done to the utmost severity.

This passage is thoroughly representative of Congreve's concern in the dedication with matters which we would consider technical and structural in a fairly narrow sense—what he calls the 'Mechanical part' of his comedy. Significantly, there is a similar emphasis in Dryden's poem of commendation. He includes wit among the comedy's excellences, along with 'easy Dialogue' and 'Courtship', but his main concern is to present Congreve as a 'new Vitruvius', a master of design whose achievement is most fittingly expressed in a metaphor drawn from architecture.

> Firm *Dorique* Pillars found Your solid Base:
> The Fair *Corinthian* Crowns the higher Space;
> Thus all below is Strength, and all above is Grace.
>
> [ll. 17–19]

The claim made by Congreve in the dedication—and I think we can accept it in this case as an honest one, although the dramatist was capable at other times of critical disingenuity—is that he had set out with the express intention of writing a play that would deserve respect as a work of literature quite apart from its success or lack of it in the theatre, 'a true and regular Comedy'. His care is especially evident in his observance of the unities which he has indeed maintained with 'utmost severity'. To satisfy 'the dreadfull men of Learning', the first and evidently most formidable of six classes of playgoer addressed in the epilogue, a comedy also needed to include 'Instruction' among its aims and Congreve is careful to bring to our attention that he had designed the fable to express a moral, a statement which must have seemed to come a little oddly from the creator of Bellmour and Vainlove. Clearly this has been an undertaking of some solemnity and one that makes *The Old Batchelour* by contrast seem a very insub-stantial enterprise. Indeed Congreve has harsh words for those who welcomed the earlier play but looked coolly upon its successor.

When we turn from the dedication to the play itself it is not hard to appreciate that an audience who were expecting a comedy in the vein of *The Old Batchelour* might have found *The Double Dealer*, or at least its opening, something of a surprise. At curtain rise, just as in *The Old Batchelour*, we are introduced to two wits, but they are not, as in the earlier play, caught at full stretch in an exchange of epigrams. Careless has just made his escape from a dinner-party at which the fools have grown noisy. (' . . . If a man must endure the noise of words without Sence, I think the Women have the more Musical Voices, and become Nonsence better.') Mellefont has followed Careless out of the room, not in order to bandy similes but to explain a complex personal predicament. In the course of his exposition it emerges that Mellefont is on the point—and as far as we can tell in a spirit of complete equanimity—of entering into marriage. Even more surprisingly, when he had been visited that morning in bed by another lady who had 'omitted nothing, that the most violent Love could urge, or tender words express', he had resolutely rejected her proffered charms. Coming from a Vainlove who would have done so on grounds of super-refined good taste, or possibly super-refined malice, this would have been perfectly acceptable; however, the excuses pleaded in this case are 'Honour and nearness of Blood', grounds which would hardly have deterred Vainlove and certainly not Bellmour, with his conviction 'the deeper the Sin the sweeter'. Indeed if it were not that a little afterwards we find Mellefont proposing his wife-to-be's stepmother as a target for his friend's powers of seduction we might very easily doubt whether he was a wit at all. As readers, and therefore more privileged in the matter, we will already have encountered Congreve's description of him as 'an Open-hearted Honest Man, who has an entire Confidence in one whom he takes to be his Friend, and whom he has obliged to be so', a description that is difficult to reconcile with the notion of the wit implicit in *The Old Batchelour*, where to be deceived, on whatever terms, is to be a gull, and confidence in others, as the sad case of Heartwell shows, the supreme act of folly.

Before he has got properly into his explanation, Mellefont is interrupted by the arrival on the scene of a third character, Brisk. His talk is 'pretty and Metaphorical', his phrases sprightly enough, and he displays a commendable facility in the sort of verbal games that Bellmour and Vainlove played so perfectly. However, he is

not welcome, and Careless and Mellefont cannot be drawn to join
with him in a wit duel, although he tries several times to entice them.
Instead, it is clear from the moment of his entry that they regard
him as an offensive pest. Such an attitude expressed towards such an
object is far from unfamiliar in Restoration comedy; quite a number
of plays include among their characters a would-be wit who imagines
himself to be one of the *beaux esprits* but is regarded by them, although
they humour him, as no better than a fool—Sparkish in Wycherley's
The Country Wife will serve as an example. However, in such a
situation in cognate plays, one would at least expect the real wits to
be witty in the presence of the sham-wit. They might insult him to
his face, certainly, but with elegance and ingenuity. Mellefont and
Careless do not react this way. Careless is particularly terse and reserved.
When Brisk charges him with 'always spoiling Company by leaving
it' which is ultimately a compliment, Careless retorts with a blunt
'And thou art always spoiling Company by coming into't.' and from
then on will hardly spare him a single word. In fact, over the play as a
whole Mellefont's and Careless's quota of 'fine things' is distinctly
meagre. And yet they are wits—although they never make the claim
themselves. The other characters certainly regard them as such, and
Brisk is prepared to go as far as to describe Mellefont as 'the Soul
of Conversation, the very Essence of Wit, and Spirit of Wine', and
to swear that there were not 'three good things said; or one, understood' since he had left the table. It is just that, prima-donna-like,
they seem perversely determined not to display their paces.

Brisk is supported in his pretences to wit by a brainless aristocrat,
Lord Froth, the poetical Lady Froth, and the persuadable Lady Plyant.
Here is the first pair in full flight with him:

Brisk. Who, my Lady *Toothless*; O, she's a mortifying
Spectacle; she's always chewing the Cud like an old *Yew*.
Cynthia. Fie Mr. *Brisk*, 'tis *Eringo's* for her Cough.
Lady Froth. I have seen her take 'em half chew'd out of her
Mouth, to Laugh, and then put 'em in again—Foh.
Lord Froth. Foh.
Lady Froth. Then she's always ready to Laugh when *Sneer*
offers to speak—And sits in expectation of his no Jest, with
her Gums bare, and her Mouth open.—
Brisk. Like an Oyster at low Ebb, I'gad———ha, ha, ha.

[III.i.567–76]

This passage is one of a number in the play in which Congreve mercilessly and at the same time very amusingly guys those for whom the great game of wit has become trivialized into mere scandal- and simile-mongering. By the terms of earlier Restoration comedy they are fools posing as wits and proclaiming their folly through the ineptness of their imitation. As far as the verbal mechanics are concerned the imitation can on occasions be quite an acceptable one, an indication perhaps that the whole thing is becoming too familiar and formulaic, but there is no sign of the other attributes that for the true wit make the game so much more than a game—his insight into the motives of others, and his mastery of the skills of social manipulation. Looking at Mr. Brisk and the Froths we may even find a certain reassuring innocence to the spectacle—they would never be able to turn the arts of the game to the malevolent ends pursued by a Dorimant, a Horner, or a Vainlove.

Placed beside such choice pieces of folly, the men who could if they wished play the game with genuine point and distinction, Careless and Mellefont, have acquired an oddly harassed air and have retreated from all obvious forms of self-display. They are true wits trapped in a world of false wits who have devalued the role to a point where the genuine adepts prefer to disclaim it. 'There are times,' Mellefont warns Careless, 'When Sense may be unseasonable, as well as Truth. Prithee do thou wear none to day; but allow *Brisk* to have Wit, that thou may'st seem a Fool.' Here Congreve is looking rather wryly at a life style that his previous comedy for all its frivolity had taken very seriously indeed. He is also letting us know that the notion of wit, and the hierarchy of attributes constructed around this, will be of considerably less importance to *The Double Dealer* than they had been to its predecessor. However witty Mellefont may be, he is not the brilliant libertine wit of earlier Restoration comedy. His primary virtue is not, perhaps, his wit at all, so much as his *honnêteté*. He is a man of the world—more justly a man *in* the world—who would like to make that world a saner and more agreeable place for others as well as for himself. In the last analysis, good or bad is going to prove more important to the play than sharp or dull.

II

It should be clear now that *The Double Dealer* is a comedy of quite another kind from *The Old Batchelour*; however, the differences so

far discussed are not necessarily the fundamental ones. For what
sets the play most strikingly apart from its predecessor is firstly the
thing to which Congreve draws our attention in his dedication—that
it is a comedy with a very carefully contrived *plot*—and secondly
that it is a comedy about a family.

The first of these two points requires special stress in that it is one
that twentieth century critics have tended to shy away from. What
Congreve presents to us is first and foremost an action, an action
complete with *protasis, epitasis*, and *catastrophe*, as recommended by
Donatus, *peripetea* as extolled by Aristotle, and a terminal *anagnorisis*
according to the practice of Plautus and Terence. It is only in the
scenes of conversation among the fools—the Froths, the Plyants and
their attendant gallants—that he is able to allow himself liberty as
a creator of character, and the effect of these scenes within the play
is, in any case, very much one of light relief. We tend to be unsympathetic towards this emphasis on plot because we look down on art-
forms which lay stress on action *qua* action, seeing farce, which is
ideally all action, as the least significant form of comedy, and melodrama, which stands in roughly the same relationship to tragedy as
farce to comedy, as beneath serious consideration. (Or we used to
anyway; there are signs that for melodrama at least the situation is
beginning to change.) Instinctively we look in art for universals,
whereas narrative, except when it aspires to the condition of ritual
or allegory, does not readily yield these. From this point of view we
would probably want to reply to Congreve's claims in the dedication
for the 'strongness', 'singleness', and mechanical perfection of his
play that we do not today lay very much importance on these things
and that we require much more from comedy than a story.

We might just as easily want to complain that Congreve's plot is
not a very good one; and indeed, as even a superficial inspection will
show, it has more than its fair share of implausibilities, forced motivations, and cut-out characterization. It is possible to have read the play
quite carefully without being sure whether Lord Touchwood is a
prize ass like his friend Froth or a hasty but good man misled by
villains. The scene in V.i. where he accepts Maskwell as his heir
could only be made plausible to a modern audience by playing it as
if there were an element of homosexual attraction involved. (Not, of
course, that Congreve necessarily *wanted* it to be plausible.) Lady
Touchwood is much more clear-cut in her reactions but, once again,
is never permitted to resemble a credible human being. Her function

is as Lust and Rage to oppose the fortunes of Mellefont; once this is done she can be brushed aside as of no real consequence. Her reaction to her exposure at the end of Act V is as bare as this:

> *A great shriek from the corner of the Stage.* Lady Touchwood
> *runs out affrighted, my Lord after her, like a Parson.*
> Lady Touchwood. O I'm betray'd,——save me, help me.
> Lord Touchwood. Now what Evasion, Strumpet?
> Lady Touchwood. Stand off, let me go, and Plagues, and
> Curses seize you all.
>
> *Runs out*
[V.i.556–62]

Her farewell line recalls Malvolio's 'I'll be revenged on the whole pack of you' but it has none of its effect or its richness of implication, the reason for this being that it has no sense of a living person behind it. Even Maskwell can hardly be said to come alive with any real vividness. Seeing that he is the title character and would appear at first glance to occupy an analogous position in the play to Molière's and Jonson's great figures of vice and evil, we naturally expect him to have something of their fascination, and yet I doubt whether many readers of the play will have felt that this was so; indeed I think it is not unfair to say that put beside Volpone or Tartuffe he is rather dull. At intervals in the action he comes out and talks directly to us. Now, if ever, he should make an impression on us as an individual, yet even these passages are curiously flat and abstract. In fact they read as if they were intended as recapitulations and foreshadowings of the action rather than as revelations of character. Here is the most developed and reflective of the soliloquies:

> *Cynthia*, let
> thy Beauty gild my Crimes; and whatsoever I commit of
> Treachery or Deceit, shall be imputed to me as a Merit
> ——Treachery, what Treachery? Love cancels all the
> Bonds of Friendship, and sets Men right upon their first
> Foundations.
>
> Duty to Kings, Piety to Parents, Gratitude to Benefac-
> tors, and Fidelity to Friends, are different and particular
> Ties: But the Name of Rival cuts 'em all asunder, and is a
> general acquittance—Rival is equal, and Love like Death
> an universal Leveller of Mankind. Ha! but is there not such
> a thing as Honesty? Yes, and whosoever has it about him,

bears an Enemy in his Breast: For your honest man, as I take it, is that nice, scrupulous, conscientious Person, who will cheat no body but himself; such another Coxcomb, as your wise man, who is too hard for all the World, and will be made a Fool of by no body, but himself: Ha, ha, ha. Well for Wisdom and Honesty, give me Cunning and Hypocrisie; oh 'tis such a pleasure, to angle for fair-faced Fools! then that hungry Gudgeon Credulity, will bite at any thing———Why, let me see, I have the same Face, the same Words and Accents, when I speak what I do think; and when I speak what I do not think—the very same— and dear dissimulation is the only Art, not to be known from Nature.

[II.i.440–64]

This is fine theatrical rhetoric and one can see how a Betterton could hold an audience entranced with it, but once again the character remains obstinately at the level of the turn: he is a Villain, much as Lady Touchwood is a Jealous Woman. Certainly he is a very smooth, a very adroit, a sublimely villainous Villain; but that is only to make him more of the same, not to give him any real individuality as a comic personage. At the end of the play, when the action has run its course and the obstacles to the marriage of Cynthia and Mellefont are finally overcome, Maskwell disappears even more completely than Lady Touchwood. For him there is not even the indulgence of a line of defiance, merely a round of abuse from the other characters— 'thou wonder of all Falsehood', 'Disease to my sight', 'manifold Villain', 'Miracle of Ingratitude'—and the bare stage direction '*They carry out* Maskwell, *who hangs down his head.*' One is tempted to see him as a personified circumstance rather than as a realized character (though Betterton would no doubt have convinced us otherwise).

In passing this judgement I must make the qualification that must attend all such judgements, that as long as a play is still a challenge to actors and producers there is always the possibility of a revelation. Having made this concession, however, it is difficult to avoid the conclusion that with the exception of Mellefont and Cynthia the characters of the upper plot have been cruelly stinted of their share of the life which appears so abundantly in Brisk, the Froths, and the Plyants. The reason for this is quite clearly Congreve's overriding and, as the dedication shows, perfectly conscious concern with effects of narrative and situation, and our next question must therefore be to ask what the dramatic point may be—whether the action exists purely and solely as a series of agreeable frissons without any real relevance to human experience, or whether we are able to give it richer meaning as emblem, as allegory, or as ritual?

III

At this stage I would like to return to the other new development in *The Double Dealer* mentioned at the beginning of the preceding section, that it is a play about a family. In a short while I will be suggesting that the thinness of some of the individual portraits is in some measure an effect of this, however, the most immediately important thing is that it allows us to establish links between Congreve's comedy and a much older dramatic tradition in which there is a similar concentration on plot and situation at the expense of other kinds of interest. We have already seen Congreve appealing to the canons of classical criticism; it is also possible to see him as imitating the models of classical comedy, or at least the part of it which is known as the 'New Comedy'—that of the Greek Menander and his Roman imitators Plautus and Terence—as opposed to the 'old' comedy of Aristophanes.[2] Greek drama in general laid great stress on the conduct of narrative while circumscribing character through the convention of the mask, Aristotle's famous eulogy of *Oedipus Tyrannus* invoking very similar critical priorities to those cited in his own justification by Congreve in the dedication to *The Double Dealer*. In Greek tragedy the course of the action would be known to the audience before the play began and could not be radically altered by the dramatist; the art was to appear in the ordering and disposing of it. The New Comedy was freer in that its plots with one or two exceptions were not mythological, but it exhibits a kinship with the type of tragedy represented by Oedipus in that it tends to be a comedy of action and situation, and, more specifically, a comedy of delusion, with the characters clearly classified as either deceivers or deceived. A similar pattern is visible in *The Double Dealer*.

A representative example of the ancient comedy which will help illuminate its influence on Congreve's play is the *Mostellaria* of Plautus

[2] For further information on the stock characters of Graeco-Roman comedy and their influence on English drama see Roger Hosley, 'The Formal Influence of Plautus and Terence' in *Elizabethan Theatre*, Stratford-upon-Avon Studies 9 (London, 1966), pp. 131–46.

based on a lost Greek play by Philemon. The initial situation is that of a supposedly well-behaved young man left in charge of the family home while his father goes on a journey who betrays his trust by borrowing money to buy a slave girl, freeing her, and making her his mistress. When news arrives that the father is returning, the lovers and their friends retire into the house, leaving the man slave, Tranio, outside with orders to prevent his master from discovering what has happened. The rest of the play is taken up with a series of ingenious stratagems by which Tranio attempts to deceive the father as to the real situation. The play ends in the collapse of the deceptions but with no more than a token resolution of the initial conflict of father and son. The comedy of the piece resides almost entirely in the trickery and inventiveness of Tranio, which is to say in narrative and situation, certainly not character. Comparison with *The Double Dealer* is illuminating insofar as this as well is a play about a trickster and likewise one whose dramatic interest derives from the spectacle of people acting under the influence of delusion. It is equally, in at least a metaphorical sense, a play about the possession of a house and the passing down of power and status from one generation to the next. In the Graeco-Roman play the process is followed only as far as the son's first surreptitious experiment with the right to authority and ownership. Later there must be a further stage involving the acceptance of citizenship in the city-state and, concomitant upon this, marriage to the daughter of another citizen. In this connection it should be borne in mind that Mellefont's marriage is crucial to the continued existence of a noble house as well as to himself and Cynthia.

As an example of the most common type of ancient comedy, which follows this process of transition through to its conclusion and points explicitly to its social significance, we might take the *Andria* of Congreve's beloved Terence, based on a play by Menander. The characters and the situation are similar—a young man is in conflict with his father over his love for a girl who, because she is not a citizen of Athens, is not considered suitable to be his wife. Once more the problem is to deceive the father over the son's real intentions, a task which is again, as generally in ancient comedy, deputed to the 'wily slave', here named Davus. In this case there is also a counterplot on the father's part which leads to rather more intricate complications and rather more varied crises than arise in the *Mostellaria*. There is also a proper reconciliation, brought about by an *anagnorisis* or unexpected discovery in which it is revealed that the girl is not after all a poor stranger from Andros but the daughter of an Athenian citizen and the sister of the girl originally chosen by the father as his son's bride.

The most interesting points of similarity between the *Andria* and *The Double Dealer* are that both centre on whether or not an impending marriage is to take place and that both are concerned with division within a family and the consequences of that division to a society whose power structures are transmitted through inheritance. This theme is in fact fundamental to ancient comedy, as are the highly stereotyped characters—the autocratic father, the disobedient son, the deceitful slave, the suffering heroine, the braggart, the parasite, the jealous courtesan—most of whom have counterparts in Congreve's play. Maskwell in particular has many features of the 'wily slave' whose task, as we have seen, was likewise one of fomenting and multiplying delusions among his masters. Maskwell's status is essentially a servile one; Mellefont treats him as a friend and equal but assumes in return an almost feudal devotion on Maskwell's part to the interests of the house of Touchwood. 'He has Obligations of Gratitude, to bind him to me', he explains to Careless, the substance of these obligations being that 'his Dependance upon my Uncle is through my means' [I.i.149–50]. More telling is Lord Touchwood's own comment in V.i. : 'Sure I was born to be controuled by those I should Command: my very Slaves will shortly give me Rules how I shall govern them.' Maskwell, who is on stage when this remark is made, has been one of these slaves, the very model of a helpful Davus or Tranio, although by this point he has received his manumission and with it a promise of the honours due to the rightful heir. *The Double Dealer* can also be seen as following the ancient conception of the *process* of comedy in that it is a drama of deception whose immediate theatrical impact lies largely in the spectacle of people acting on notions about the nature of reality which are false and whose resolution is achieved by a completely arbitrary undeceiving—the *anagnorisis*.

Once we become aware of Congreve's inheritance from the New Comedy we have gone a good way towards explaining those features of *The Double Dealer* which set it apart from *The Old Batchelour* and the two later comedies. The crucial point here is that both *The Double Dealer* and its ancient models are plays about the ways in which a family decays or somehow proves unsatisfactory in one generation and is renewed more hopefully in the next. This is likewise, and again with help from Plautus and Terence, a central theme of Shake-spearean comedy, *The Tempest* and *A Winter's Tale* being the two most splendid examples. In each of these two plays the old generation is divided by bitterness and envy. In one, brother has turned against brother and uncle against niece, in the other husband against wife and father against child. In both, the eventual marriage of the children is not just a knitting-up of old enmities but a renewal of the families as social organisms and a promise that they will continue to exist into the future.

In Congreve the pattern of one generation attempting what another has failed in is even clearer: the marriages of the older couples are simply falling apart in front of our eyes. While we watch, two cuckolds are made and a third husband separates from his wife for ever. Our attention, therefore, as in Shakespeare, is not directed towards the fate of a particular pair of lovers but that of a whole family, a dynastic fate. Where Congreve parts company with Shakespeare and reveals himself as closer to the authentic spirit of the New Comedy is that his family is shown to us as part of a society and as playing a significant role in that society so that the dynastic fate becomes a communal fate. A similar awareness will be found in the Graeco-Roman plays. The concern in Plautus and Terence is not simply for the family but for the city-state based on restrictive hereditary citizenship of which the family is the foundation. The real disobedience of the son in *Andria* does not consist in his wanting to marry a poor girl when his father has chosen a rich one for him but that she is a fatherless stranger from the island of Andros. Once she has found her father and he is an Athenian the objection disappears. Thus marriage is important in ancient comedy not simply because audiences love a lover but because the continued existence of the city-state depends on the smooth passing down of the responsibility for its maintenance. To marry an alien, or wilfully not to marry which was the problem in the *Mostellaria* (and is still the problem in *Portnoy's Complaint*), is in small or greater measure to aid in the dissolution of an embattled society. Conversely, to make the right marriage in a society which is in danger of dissolution, submergence, or genetic dilution may be an act of crucial, even heroic, importance like the mating of some near-extinct bird.

When we apply these ideas to *The Double Dealer*, the love relationship and the concluding marriage assume a new kind of dramatic weight. The play takes place in the London house of Lord Touchwood where a select group of relatives and friends has gathered to celebrate the marriage of Mellefont and Cynthia. These people are connected to each other by elaborate and often conflicting patterns of affinity and antagonism, rather like atoms in a complex and unstable molecule. In the first place most of them are related by blood or marriage. Mellefont is Lord Touchwood's nephew, apparently through the female line; Lady Touchwood is consequently Mellefont's aunt-by-marriage; she is also the sister of Sir Paul Plyant, which makes her Cynthia's aunt and the sister-in-law of Lady Plyant, Cynthia's step-mother. When the marriage takes place these genealogical links will become even tighter in that Lord Touchwood will now be Cynthia's uncle by-marriage, Sir Paul, Mellefont's father-in-law, Lady Plyant his mother-in-law, and Lady Touchwood his aunt-by-marriage on the female side as she is already on the male.

These relationships comprise the 'official' structure of the family on which its strength and cohesion depend; however, counterpointing them is a second set of relationships created out of sexual attraction and revulsion which are to a large extent working in opposition to the bonds created by kinship. Thus Lady Touchwood, aunt to Cynthia and aunt-by-marriage to Mellefont, is herself in love with him and is working to prevent the marriage (that would draw the kinship bonds even tighter between them) by fomenting antagonism between him and his uncle and parents-in-law-to-be. She is simultaneously deceiving her husband with a lover, Maskwell, not a member of the family but an outsider scheming to replace the rightful heir as the recipient of Lord Touchwood's fortune and the hand of Cynthia. At the same time as all this is happening, Lady Plyant, already related to Mellefont through her husband and Lady Touchwood and on the verge of becoming his mother-in-law, is showing signs of being herself attracted to him, although she is soon diverted from this by his friend Careless. In each of the cases indicated, sexual passion or sexual jealousy is working in the opposite direction to the supposedly cohesive force of kinship. Things are made even more critical by the circumstance that Lord Touchwood is childless and that Sir Paul has only one child, Cynthia. Thus on the marriage of Mellefont and Cynthia depends the continuance of the no doubt ancient and hon-ourable houses of Plyant and Touchwood, a considerable fortune, and possibly a title. Should the marriage not take place, should Mask-well win, the kinship bond would snap altogether and the family cease to exist as a genealogical unit: at the height of its prosperity it is in a position of acute dynastic vulnerability, and through it the caste of which it is part, the aristocracy, is also vulnerable.

The Double Dealer, then, is not just a comedy about a pair of lovers, nor just a comedy about a family, but a comedy about a dynasty and ultimately a class. Its action is a symbolic enactment of class antagonism. The dynastic vulnerability of the houses of Touchwood and Plyant has attracted an enemy in the person of Maskwell. Maskwell is not himself an aristocrat but an infiltrator from the level of the declining lower gentry, or more probably the bourgeoisie— a male Pamela in a black wig. (This point could be emphasized in performance by having Maskwell lapse into a regional accent for his soliloquies.) He is a threat to the 'genealogical' family in two ways. In the first place there is the possibility that he could make Lady Touchwood pregnant, thus driving out the true heir. This would not have destroyed the family as a structural unit but by introducing base blood would effectively have corrupted it. (For the moment we will accept what I assume to have been Congreve's own point of view on such matters.) The second aim is the more daring one of himself coming to occupy the place of Mellefont as the head and renewer of the family. Had he succeeded in this, the corruption would not have been restricted to the one particular family. Like the ancient city-state, the seventeenth century aristocracy was a socially exclusive group built up of a restricted number of related families. Anything that damaged a particular family would also damage the class; or, to use Maskwell's own words at the close of Act I—'One Minute, gives Invention to Destroy,/What to Rebuild, will a whole Age Employ.' Moreover, anything that damages the class will also, at least in the view of that class, damage society. The transfer of aristocratic status to a bourgeois interloper would affect the way in which wealth and power were used and the people on whom they were used. The theme is in this respect similar to that of *Tartuffe* or of Wilde's *An Ideal Husband*, the capitulation of a noble household to a malicious intriguer from another class who will divert their resources to selfseeking ends. It is interesting that Careless is not fooled about Maskwell. He knows there is something wrong with him, although he can justify it only by pleading that he is 'a little Superstitious in Physiognomy'. (An Edwardian Careless would presumably have felt that Maskwell 'was not quite a gentleman'.) Perhaps it is Mellefont's dynastic position that has made him too trusting in this case; both he and the Touchwoods see Maskwell as their creature, a kind of extension of themselves and their own desires; they do this because their model of social relationships is still, rather anachronistically, one that sees service to the dynasty as the highest human satisfaction. It does not enter their heads that the servant could aspire to replace his masters, any more than it does Volpone's that he would be betrayed by Mosca. It may also be part of the moral that Mellefont, who was responsible for letting the wolf into the lambfold to start with, should be marked down as his first dinner.

Once this kind of implication is made clear, certain aspects of the play begin at once to make more sense. Congreve's regression to Terentian formulas is no longer wilful anachronism but a recognition that the ancient writers shared his concern with the disparity between the bonds created by sexual affinity and those desirable to ensure the transmission of social privilege and communal identity. This recognition does not necessarily make the action of the play more plausible but it does give new point to Maskwell's incredible plots, overheard soliloquies, and arch self-confessions. These things would be intolerable coming from a supposedly realistic character, but he is not such a character. He is a bad dream from the subconscious of the aristocracy.

IV

To say these things is, as I mentioned earlier, to accept the values of the besieged class without question and to condemn the aggressor by their light. So once again from a modern point of view there is room for complaint. There will not be many among the readers of this book, I imagine, who would share Congreve's unquestioning faith in the perpetual right to power and privilege of the members of the English House of Lords. In the final tableau of *The Double Dealer*, Lord Touchwood and Mellefont stand in triumphant righteousness over the cringing figure of the faithless servant, the class-enemy who has struck through deceit at the very basis of their social existence. To us their postures seem strained and a little ridiculous but there is no reason to believe that Congreve intended us to find them so; the bold melodramatic emblem was not debased for him, as it is for us, by centuries of misuse. What the tableau presents is a vision of the essential rightness of things. We are suddenly aware that Maskwell never really had a chance in the first place. It was not the aristocracy he was fighting but Providence.

To give assent to the action of *The Double Dealer*, then, is also to give assent to the system of government by hereditary oligarchy, a fact that explains many of our difficulties with the play. And yet by a rather curious paradox the assent is asked only for the class, not for the individuals who comprise it. By whom after all is the aristocracy represented? By the families of Froth, Touchwood, and Plyant; by men who are dupes, fools, and bores, and by women who with only one exception are hypocritical, affected, and rather pointlessly promiscuous. It will be salutary at this stage to catch each of the principal offenders at a characteristic moment. Firstly the Froths:

> *Lord Froth.* Hee, hee, hee, my Dear, have you done——— wont you joyn with us, we were laughing at my Lady *Whifler*, and Mr. *Sneer*.
> *Lady Froth.*—Ay my Dear—were you? Oh filthy Mr. *Sneer*; he's a nauseous figure, a most fulsamick Fop, Foh—he spent two days together in going about *Covent-Garden* to suit the lining of his Coach with his complexion.
> *Lord Froth.* O silly! yet his Aunt is as fond of him, as if she had brought the Ape into the World her self.
>   [III.i.558–66]

next Sir Paul:

> *Sir Paul.* He? And wilt thou bring a Grandson at 9 Months end—He? A brave Chopping Boy.—I'll settle a Thousand pound a Year upon the Rogue as soon as ever he looks me in the Face, I will Gads-bud. I'm overjoy'd to think I have any of my Family that will bring Children into the World. For I would fain have some resemblance of my self in my Posterity, he *Thy*? Can't you contrive that affair Girl? Do gads-bud, think on thy old Father; Heh? Make the young Rogue as like as you can.
> *Cynthia.* I'm glad to see you so merry, Sir.
>   [IV.i.223–32]

and, finally, Lady Touchwood:

> *Lady Touchwood.* Death, do you dally with my Passion? Insolent Devil! But have a care,———provoke me not; For, by the Eternal Fire, you shall not scape my Vengance. ———Calm Villain! How unconcern'd he stands, Confessing Treachery and Ingratitude! Is there Vice more black!———O I have Excuses, Thousands for my Faults; Fire in my Temper, Passions in my Soul, apt to every provocation; oppressed at once with Love, and with Despair.
>   [I.i.320–27]

What even the briefest of glances makes clear is that, whatever the official moral of play, the actual presentation of aristocrats and their hangers-on is hostile and satiric. The point was not lost on Congreve's sternest critic among his contemporaries, Jeremy Collier, who chose to present the play as an outright attack upon the aristocracy:

> And the *Double Dealer* is particularly remarkable. There are but *Four* Ladys in this *Play*, and *Three* of the biggest of them are *Whores*. A Great Compliment to Quality, to tell them there is not above a quarter of them Honest.[3]

The spirit that presents the aristocrats to us is critical, taking a malicious delight in the exposure of their heartlessness, the futility and narcissism of their self-absorbed games, whether love or epic poetry, and their sublime incapacity to realize that others might suffer as a result of their follies, or if they did suffer, that this would somehow matter.

And yet having given his general assent to the system, Congreve cannot allow his particular criticisms to go too far. It is, after all, these creatures who at the end of the play are assembled to stand in judgement on manifest evil and on whose behalf we are called to rejoice in the exposure of the baffled enemy. The disparity at this point is one of tone as well as of point of view: the effect of the chatter of Lady Froth and Mr Brisk alongside the melodramatic rhetoric of Lord and Lady Touchwood is a striking though not necessarily an unsuccessful one. There is certainly some degree of ironical judgement implied; however, it is not one that qualifies the other implications of the finale in any serious way. We take the disparity of levels in our stride without feeling any compulsion to resolve it. Even as he assails the persons, Congreve is making obeisance to the institution within which these persons have their being and its time-sanctioned dignity. The underlying assent to what they stand for serves to mitigate the effect of their follies. Moreover, if they are fools, they are certainly not dull fools. They possess a confidence, a power to exhilarate, a comic élan to which, in the theatre at least, we will respond with active delight. Even in their moments of self-exposure there is somehow a sense of contented complicity about them, the perfect innocence of the buffoon who does not know he is a buffoon or, if he does, does not care. Despite the weight of the implied criticism and the self-conscious moralism of the fable, Congreve is never prepared to call

[3] Jeremy Collier, *A Short View of the Immorality and Profaneness of the English Stage*, 3rd edn. (London, 1698), p. 12.

the pleasure of these children in their games seriously into question—which is, after all, exactly what we would expect from a man not himself of the aristocracy but whose life was spent in their shadow, the son of the steward of the great Earl of Burlington, the commoner who was to end his days the lover of a duchess. He may dislike them but he is incapable of conceiving a life which does not have them at its centre.

V

So Congreve's attitude towards the class which is the subject of his play is not a simple one. They may be mocked but at the same time their very existence is a reassurance, an inevitability. Nor should we forget that in two cases Congreve's portrait is a strongly favourable one. Mellefont and Cynthia belong to the same class as the Plyants, the Froths, and the Touchwoods, but they are nonetheless allowed to earn our respect and in a measure our affection. Insofar as they are also the point of biological renewal for family and caste, the exception is a particularly important one. In contrast with the unbridled extravagance which surrounds them, their simplicity and frankness, the sense of a muted but honest affection, and their charitable tolerance of the eccentricities of others make them perhaps the most immediately likeable of all Congreve's lovers. Their relationship is mercifully uncomplicated. They are in love, they wish to marry. They are aware of the dynastic role they must play and have no illusions about the concessions it will force on them, but they have faith that their personal affection will be strong enough to survive this and that a workable compromise between the personal and the social role is possible.

The cheering thing about them is that they can retain confidence in the strength of their affection while at the same time seeing very clearly and very steadily into the reality of the lives that are being lived so extravagantly but so unsatisfactorily around them. Of the two it is perhaps Cynthia who is the keener sighted. As the patient listener to the ramblings of Lady Froth, the witness of her father's imbecilities, and the dutiful endurer of her patronizing stepmother, she has been able to make a thorough appraisal of the evidence. Yet she is not embittered by it. She can even find humour in it, an encouraging sign. 'That my poor Father, should be so very silly', is her only comment on an exceptionally blatant piece of manipulation by Lady Plyant and it is exactly the right comment. Lady Plyant is

Ec

simply not the sort of person one gets seriously upset about; neither perhaps is Sir Paul, but of course he is Cynthia's father and is fond of her and she spontaneously returns this fondness, even to the extent of accepting his parental power of veto.

But it is not merely follies and Maskwells that pose the threat: there is marriage itself as displayed for her inspection in the persons of her father, her stepmother, the Touchwoods and the Froths. Her doubts about the match at the beginning of Act IV are partly due to a fear of what she has seen marriage do to people. Mellefont and she are helpless and isolated idealists in a world of middle-aged liars and charlatans and know that they must some day be middle-aged themselves and cannot help asking whether they are fated to be liars and charlatans as well. Must Cynthia harden helplessly into one of these brilliant, self-proclaiming creatures? Must she too have her Mr. Brisk, her Careless, her Maskwell? Is this what marriage must bring? At a crucial point in the play she puts the question directly to Melle-font:

> *Cynthia.* I'm thinking, that tho' Marriage makes Man and Wife One Flesh, it leaves 'em still Two Fools; and they become more Conspicuous by setting off one another.
> *Mellefont.* That's only when Two Fools meet, and their follies are oppos'd.
> *Cynthia.* Nay, I have known Two Wits meet, and by the opposition of their Wits, render themselves as ridiculous as Fools. 'Tis an odd Game we're going to Play at: What think you of drawing Stakes, and giving over in time?
> *Mellefont.* No, hang't, that's not endeavouring to Win, because it's possible we may lose; since we have Shuffled and Cutt, let's e'en turn up Trump now.
> *Cynthia.* Then I find its like Cards, if either of us have a good Hand, it is an Accident of Fortune.
> *Mellefont.* No, Marriage is rather like a Game of Bowls, Fortune indeed makes the match, and the Two nearest, and sometimes the Two farthest are together, but the Game depends entirely upon Judgment.
> *Cynthia.* Still it is a Game, and Consequently one of us must be a Loser.
>
> [II.i.155–69]

Mellefont is much more cheerful about it all, indeed the terms of the play hardly allow the issue to be pursued too single-mindedly. He has confidence in the honesty of his own feelings and is prepared to assume their permanence. His reply to her last objection is a simple 'Not at all; only a Friendly Tryal of Skill, and the Winnings to be Shared between us.' It is possible to see Mellefont's confidence as part of the same fundamental innocence that has made him the dupe of Maskwell—but then Cynthia does not doubt his readiness to trust, it is his and her own capacity not to abuse trust which is the real issue. Perhaps his future is indeed to be a betrayed Touchwood, a garrulous Froth, and at the last a doddering Plyant. On the other hand perhaps not: there is the reassurance that they have survived what they have and certainly the object lessons in folly and villainy presented to them have been of the most instructive kind. We have faith in them as we leave them, no longer just Mellefont and Cynthia but the inheritors and renewers of the houses of Touchwood and Plyant, and perhaps a little more faith as well, although this is much more problematical, in the kind of social order they stood for.

4

Love for Love

The Double Dealer, although in no sense a realistic play, had been one whose central concerns were social and which had a precise social focus in the life-style of the aristocracy, or, if we are to speak with complete precision, that of the lower stratum of the barony and the upper of the baronetcy. With *Love for Love*, Congreve has descended to a world of country knights with sons at sea, wealthy recluses devoted to the study of the occult, female fortune-hunters, spend-thrift heirs, and beautiful, wealthy wards—a world which is prophetic in many ways of the 'eccentric squire' class of Victorian fiction. It must also be stated that it is a world without very many points of contact with the real one. The earlier plays had not pretended to show life as it was, but had accepted that the canons of probability which govern choice in the everyday world also applied in the world of the drama—which meant that characters who placed any considerable degree of reliance on others usually came to disaster. In *Love for Love*, we find ourselves snatched away from the Hobbesian battleground to a considerably kinder sphere. This does not mean that possessiveness, bullying, greed, ego-assertion, filial ingratitude, parental tyranny, and lust after other people's bodies and cash are any less evident than in the other plays—simply that these activities have somehow become less threatening and that we have ceased to be apprehensive about their consequences. What we see in *Love for Love* is in fact a movement away from a detached, judicial, and, as Brian Gibbons has suggested, Jonsonian approach towards the Shakespearean vision of comedy as a holiday world of liberated vitality.[1] This means in practical terms that

[1] Brian Gibbons, 'Congreve's *The Old Batchelour* and Jonsonian Comedy' in *William Congreve*, ed. Brian Morris (London: 1972), pp. 3–20.

it is now possible for characters to take risks of a kind that would have been impossible or at least reprehensible in the earlier plays and see them come off, even to the extent of trusting another human being with everything one has and seeing that trust not abused.

The main consequence of this is that the play cannot really be classified as a social comedy. There is little of the close attention to the minutiae of personal interaction that we have seen in *The Old Batchelour* and will see again in *The Way of the World*. The dynastic themes of *The Double Dealer* are formally present to some degree but are given none of the dramatic weight they receive in that play. Instead, Congreve has turned to a remarkably pure form of the comedy of courtship, a comic mode which can be exemplified for our purposes by Shakespeare's *Love's Labour's Lost*, and two Caroline plays, James Shirley's *The Lady of Pleasure* and John Fletcher's *The Elder Brother* (the last of these the source of a number of specific borrowings, among them the phrase 'love for love'). The thing linking these three plays with Congreve's is a view of courtship which sees it not simply as a source of effortless empathies, but as a process of learning or school of civility in which the man is pupil and the woman the teacher. The same ideal lies at the heart of the love poetry of Petrarch and Dante and of the Elizabethan sonnet sequences. For the Italian poets, love conceived in this sense could be presented not simply as a school of civility, but as an induction into the highest values of a civilization, and even in Congreve's much more prosaic age a little of the grandeur of the older conception remained:

> Love, studious how to please, improves our Parts,
> With polish'd Manners, and adorns with Arts.
> Love first invented Verse, and form'd the Rhime,
> The Motion measur'd, harmoniz'd the Chime;
> To lib'ral Acts inlarg'd the narrow-Soul'd,
> Soften'd the Fierce, and made the Coward Bold:
> The World when wast, he Peopled with increase,
> And warring Nations reconcil'd in Peace.
>
> ['Cymon and Iphigenia', ll. 31–8]

Dryden's poem (based on Boccaccio) from which these lines come presents the heuristic vision of courtship in its purest form. Cymon, the rustic 'Man-Beast' who has resisted all attempts to educate him to knowledge and nobility, is transformed by the power of love into a model of the social virtues:

Inspir'd by Love, whose Business is to please;
He Rode, he Fenc'd, he mov'd with graceful Ease,
More fam'd for Sense, for courtly Carriage more,
Than for his brutal Folly known before.

[ll. 222–5]

The Elder Brother has a similar theme. Charles, a scholarly recluse, is
on the point of making a free surrender of his right of inheritance
to his younger brother when he catches sight of Angellina and is
transformed in a similar way to Cymon and with much the same
results. In *Love for Love*, roles analogous to that of the unredeemed
Cymon are given to Ben and Prue. The transformations to be wrought
in Valentine are not quite of the same order—he is already a master
of the skills of behaviour and address—but are certainly much more
than lessons in social technique. He has to show himself capable of
undergoing a fundamental moral change, and it is only when he has
done this that he is finally acceptable to his mentor Angelica as lover
and husband.

In applying these ideas to the play, the first thing we need to observe
is that the action is built up around three sets of lessons each involving
a teacher and a pupil. At the lowest level there are Tattle's instructions
to Miss Prue in the ways of the world and in the right way of performing the role she must as a woman be prepared to adopt in this
world. Next comes Mrs. Frail's lessons to Ben, couched in the form
of example rather than of precept, and centring on the cardinal rules
of always living defensively and never trusting another human being.
The third lesson is at an altogether higher level. At the beginning of
the play Valentine is presented as a carefree rake who has exhausted
his money in his pursuit of Angelica and has only his wit to rely on
to sustain the pursuit. His basic assumption is that he can trick or
bribe her into loving him; and in holding it he is relegating her to the
status of an inferior being. Her aim is to teach him the foolishness
of this attitude and her method is to force him to the point where he
has to choose in a particularly testing way between love and money—
whether having apparently lost her love he is prepared for her sake
to lose the money too. By making the second choice he shows the
unselfishness of his love and permits Angelica to proceed to the other
part of the lesson, which is the public humiliation of Valentine's
tyrannical father, Sir Sampson.

The first of the pupils is Miss Prue, and hers is to be the most hilar-
ious lesson of all. She has inherited her ignorance of the great world

from her father Foresight, but whereas he is content to continue in this state she is eager to escape from it. In Tattle she has a teacher exactly levelled at her capacity. We meet him first in Act I when he visits Valentine and Scandal. The joke of the scene is that Tattle, while incredibly vain of his amours (which may be imaginary), insists on maintaining the pretence that he has 'never expos'd a Woman' since he 'knew what Woman was'. The incompatibility of the two aims involves him in more and more elaborate examples of verbal prestidigitation. Scandal and Valentine tempt him with the accusation (which, again, may or may not be true) that he has had a liaison with Mrs. Frail. Tattle's problem is to find out the precise formula which will allow him to lay claim to having had the lady without prejudice to his professions of inviolable secrecy. His solution is a minor triumph:

> *Tattle.* Upon my Soul *Angelica*'s a fine Woman———And so is Mrs. *Foresight*, and her Sister Mrs. *Frail*.
> *Scandal.* Yes, Mrs. *Frail* is a very fine Woman, we all know her.
> *Tattle.* Oh that is not fair.
> *Scandal.* What?
> *Tattle.* To tell.
> *Scandal.* To tell what? Why, what do you know of Mrs. *Frail*?
> *Tattle.* Who I? Upon Honour I don't know whether she be Man or Woman; but by the smoothness of her Chin, and roundness of her Lips.
> *Scandal.* No!
> *Tattle.* No.
> *Scandal.* She says otherwise.
> *Tattle.* Impossible!
> *Scandal.* Yes Faith. Ask *Valentine* else.
> *Tattle.* Why then, as I hope to be sav'd, I believe a Woman only obliges a Man to Secresie, that she may have the pleasure of telling her self.
> *Scandal.* No doubt on't. Well, but has she done you wrong, or no? You have had her? Ha?
> *Tattle.* Tho' I have more Honour than to tell first; I have more Manners than to contradict what a Lady has declar'd.
> [I.i.456–79]

As it happens there is an unwelcome surprise in store for Tattle in that Mrs. Frail is just on the point of appearing in person—but his

qualifications for life in the town are nonetheless seen to be considerable. By the time we meet Miss Prue, fresh arrived from the country,
she is already completely in thrall to these perfections:

> *Miss Prue.* Look you here, Madam then, what Mr. *Tattle* has
> giv'n me———Look you here Cousin, here's a Snuff-box;
> nay, there's Snuff in't;———here, will you have any———
> Oh good! how sweet it is———Mr. *Tattle* is all over sweet,
> his Perruke is sweet, and his Gloves are sweet.———and his
> Handkerchief is sweet, pure sweet, sweeter than Roses———
> Smell him Mother, Madam, I mean———He gave me
> this Ring for a kiss.
>
> [II.i.515–22]

It is at this point that Prue's urgent need for instruction is brought
home to Tattle, and he begins with the most elementary lesson of all:
'O fie Miss, you must not kiss and tell.' There follows a slightly
sinister scene in which Prue stands in uncomprehending simplicity
while Mrs. Foresight and Mrs. Frail make it clear to Tattle that they
would have no objection to his seducing her. (There are hints from
Mrs. Frail that Prue's eagerness for experience may be put under
even greater strain at some future date: 'Lord, what pure red and
white!———she looks so wholesome;———ne're stir, I don't know,
but I fancy, if I were a Man———'.) Tattle naturally has no objections
to the proposal nor, when the moment comes to put it into action,
does Prue. But first it is necessary for her to have a crash course in
the ways of the town, beginning with the basics. The scene that
follows is a gem of comic writing;

> *Tattle.* I must make Love to you, pretty Miss; will you let
> me make Love to you?
> *Miss Prue.* Yes, if you please.
> *Tattle* (*aside*). Frank, I Gad at least. . . .
> *Miss Prue.* Well, and how will you make Love to me———
> Come, I long to have you begin;———must I make Love
> too? You must tell me how.
> *Tattle.* You must let me speak Miss, you must not speak first;
> I must ask you Questions, and you must answer.
> *Miss Prue.* What, is it like the Catechisme?———Come then
> ask me.
> *Tattle.* De'e you think you can Love me?
> *Miss Prue.* Yes.

Tattle. Pooh, Pox, you must not say yes already; I shan't care a Farthing for you then in a twinckling.

Miss Prue. What must I say then?

Tattle. Why you must say no, or you believe not, or you can't tell——

Miss Prue. Why, must I tell a Lie then?

Tattle. Yes, if you would be well-bred. All well-bred Persons Lie——Besides, you are a Woman, you must never speak what you think: Your words must contradict your thoughts; but your Actions may contradict your words. So, when I ask you, if you can Love me, you must say no, but you must Love me too——If I tell you you are Handsome, you must deny it, and say I flatter you—— But you must think your self more Charming than I speak you:——And like me, for the Beauty which I say you have, as much as if I had it my self——If I ask you to Kiss me, you must be angry, but you must not refuse me. If I ask you for more, you must be more angry,——but more complying; and as soon as ever I make you say you'l cry out, you must be sure to hold your Tongue.

Miss Prue. O Lord, I swear this is pure,——I like it better than our old fashion'd Country way of speaking ones mind;—— and must not you lie too?

Tattle. Hum——Yes——But you must believe I speak Truth.

Miss Prue. O Gemini! well, I always had a great mind to tell Lies—but they frighted me, and said it was a sin.

Tattle. Well, my pretty Creature; will you make me happy by giving me a Kiss?

Miss Prue. No, indeed; I'm angry at you.—

Runs and kisses him

Tattle. Hold, hold, that's pretty well,—but you should not have given it me, but have suffer'd me to take it.

Miss Prue. Well, we'll do it again.

Tattle. With all my heart,—Now then my little Angel.

Kisses her.

Miss Prue. Pish.

Tattle. That's right,——again my Charmer.

Kisses again.

Miss Prue. O fie, now I can't abide you.

Tattle. Admirable! That was as well as if you had been born and bred in *Covent-Garden*, all the days of your Life;——

[II.i.588–645]

The importance of this scene is that it takes us not simply into the
school but the very kindergarten of civility. We see Miss Prue learning
a trick; then beginning to see the possibilities of the trick; then realiz-
ing it is not just a trick but a style; then finally seizing the initiative
in the exchange from Tattle's hands into her own. Viewed simply as a
lesson its substance is twofold. In the first place Prue must learn
the fundamental skill of dissimulation; next she must learn to make
use of this in order to manipulate others. Of course on a first encounter
it is not very likely that we will become specifically aware of this:
more probably we will be swept along by the sheer fun of the scene,
the teacher's delight in his pupil's quickness and the pupil's exhilaration with her new game which, when played for stakes as minimal
as the virtue of a Prue, is indeed a delightful one. But we should bear
in mind that the pattern of instruction and response which we see in
Tattle and Prue is exactly that which at a more elevated level governs
the relationship of Angelica and Valentine, and that the stakes on
that occasion are very considerable indeed.

Ben comes into the play only a scene or two later and as far as the
town is concerned is at least as great an innocent as Prue. He shares
her readiness to speak out openly and frankly on all occasions, especially
the least appropriate. The difference between them is that where
she comes equipped with nothing but country ignorance and country
morality, both of which she would sooner be without, his is sea
innocence and sea morality, and it is only the first of these which he
is prepared to surrender. He is the same dim-witted but well-disposed
creature as Sir Willfull Witwoud in *The Way of the World*, although
without any comparable opportunity to put his good disposition to
work in the service of his fellows. It is not apparent that anyone
else in the play sees him as other than a booby to be exploited; his
revenge is that he is able to retort to their insults with what the audience recognizes to be truth.

Like Prue, Ben soon finds his tutor and also like Prue that the tutor's
intentions are far from disinterested. Mrs. Foresight, having discovered
that Valentine is to be disinherited in favour of Ben, plots to break
the proposed match between Prue and Ben in order to secure the
inheritance for Frail. The first part of the scheme does not prove
difficult. By the time Prue is introduced to her intended husband
she has already had her expectations raised to a much more sublime
pitch by Tattle. The first meeting between her and Ben quickly
breaks down into a slanging match, after which he is the easiest of

conquests for Mrs. Frail who is companionably prepared to speak to him in his own sea-language.

Ben's problem is not just that he speaks the truth himself but that he assumes that other people do as well, and in this at least Prue has done nothing to disillusion him. Such trust, however, cannot be expected to survive for long. When Valentine is presented mad and it appears that he cannot be disinherited after all, Mrs. Frail decides to give her lover 'his discharge'. Her excuse is a report of a quarrel Ben has had with his father over the proposed marriage with Prue:

> *Mrs. Frail.* And were you this undutiful and graceless Wretch to your Father?
> *Ben.* Then why was he graceless first,—if I am undutiful and Graceless, why did he beget me so? I did not get my self.
> *Mrs. Frail.* O Impiety! how have I been mistaken! what an inhumane merciless Creature have I set my heart upon? O I am happy to have discover'd the Shelves and Quick-sands that lurk beneath that faithless smiling face.
>
> [IV.i.388–395]

Ben is initially bewildered by this; however even he must now realize that things cannot be all they seem, and at this point Mrs. Frail is prepared to teach by precept as well as demonstration:

> *Ben.*   What d'ee mean, after all your fair speeches, and stroaking my Cheeks, and Kissing and Hugging, what wou'd you sheer off so? wou'd you, and leave me aground?
> *Mrs. Frail.* No, I'll leave you a-drift, and go which way you will.
> *Ben.* What, are you false hearted then?
> *Mrs. Frail.* Only the Wind's chang'd.
>
> [ll.416–23]

On the whole Ben takes his disappointment well—Frail is even a little piqued at his apparent insensibility—but the encounter has been a crucial one nonetheless. He is a 'sea-calf' to one prospective mistress, a 'porpoise' to another, and a 'Fish' to his father. He has learned from this and other experiences that the inhabitants of the town are either mad or bad and is contented to return as quickly as he can to his own element. His advantage is that while he has been tricked he has not been hurt: his rich stock of sea-philosophy makes him fairly

immune to land-disappointments and as mentioned earlier he is
allowed on occasions, and without requiring the justification of
assumed madness, to tell people what he really thinks of them—a rare
and precious privilege.

Shortly after Ben receives his final lesson in town realities, Prue is
given hers. When Tattle is led to understand (falsely, as it happens)
that Angelica wishes to marry him, he is as prompt in disposing of
Prue as Frail had been in getting rid of Ben. And Prue, like Ben, takes
it rather better than one might have expected.

> *Miss Prue.*   You say you love me,
>   and you won't be my Husband. And I know you may be
>   my Husband now if you please....
> *Tattle.* O Pox, that was Yesterday, Miss, that was a great
>   while ago, Child. I have been asleep since; slept a whole
>   Night, and did not so much as dream of the matter.
> *Miss Prue.* Pshaw, O but I dream't that it was so tho.
> *Tattle.* Ay, but your Father will tell you that Dreams come
>   by Contraries, Child———O fie; what, we must not love
>   one another now———Pshaw, that would be a foolish
>   thing indeed———Fie, fie, you're a Woman now, and
>   must think of a new Man every Morning, and forget him
>   every Night———No, no, to marry, is to be a Child again,
>   and play with the same Rattle always: O fie, marrying is a
>   paw thing.
> *Miss Prue.* Well, but don't you love me as well as you did
>   last Night then?
> *Tattle.* No, no, Child, you would not have me.
> *Miss Prue.* No? Yes but I would tho.
> *Tattle.* Pshaw, but I tell you, you would not—You forget
>   you're a Woman, and don't know your own mind.
>   [V.i.228–53]

Prue still has a great deal to learn about technique; but the differences
in basic approach between her and her instructor are not as wide as
might appear. With both of them the real concern is with the thing
rather than with the person—money in his case, sex in hers. As a
consequence, Tattle after his departure comes to be devalued even more
steeply than Prue herself had been:

> I'll have a Husband; and if you
>   won't get me one, I'll get one for my self: I'll marry our
>   *Robbin* the Butler, he says he loves me, and he's a Handsome

Man, and shall be my Husband: I warrant he'll be my
Husband and thank me too, for he told me so.

[ll. 315–19]

On first sight it may seem that Prue has not learned as much as we
had thought, but given the straightforward nature of her requirements, the choice of Robin the butler over 'Lying, Foppery, Vanity,
Cowardise, Bragging, Lechery, Impotence and Ugliness' in the shape
of a 'profest Beau' is no doubt a very sensible one. (How instructive
too to learn that even the humble house of Foresight has its domestic
Maskwell!) It was rash, admittedly, of her to be quite so frank to
her father, who shows uncharacteristic practicality in sending for
Robin to sack him, but this is an error that we would not expect
her to repeat. Given the limited nature of her opportunities, and the
brevity of her tuition, Prue's progress can still be compared without
shame to that of an earlier country innocent, Margery Pinchwife.

The lessons learned by Ben and by Prue are the elementary skills
of social survival in the town. They centre around the necessity for
dissimulation and the importance of allowing for habitual dissimulation in interpreting the statements and behaviour of others. That
these though simple are not easy lessons is evident from the disaster
that overtakes the two professed masters, Tattle and Frail, lured into
totally unintended matrimony with each other. Even the experienced
Scandal still has things to learn. Having spent the night with Mrs.
Foresight he is incautious enough to mention the fact to her the
following morning and then, to compound the felony, countrified
enough to be surprised at the result:

> *Scandal.* Hush, softly——the Pleasures of last Night, my
> Dear, too considerable to be forgot so soon.
> *Mrs. Foresight.* Last Night! and what wou'd your Impudence
> infer from last night? last Night was like the Night before,
> I think.
> *Scandal.* 'S'death do you make no difference between me and
> your Husband?
> *Mrs. Foresight.* Not much,——he's superstitious; and you
> are mad in my opinion.
> *Scandal.* You make me mad——You are not serious——
> Pray recollect your self.
> *Mrs. Foresight.* O yes, now I remember, you were very
> impertinent and impudent,——and would have come to
> Bed to me.

Scandal. And did not?

Mrs. Foresight. Did not! with that face can you ask the
    Question?

Scandal. This I have heard of before, but never believ'd. I
    have been told she had that admirable quality of forgetting
    to a man's face in the morning, that she had layn with him
    all night, and denying favours with more impudence, than
    she cou'd grant 'em.—Madam, I'm your humble Servant,
    and honour you.

                                              [IV.i.316–38]

Scandal's experience shows that one's education in the ways of the
world can never be entirely complete. But it also makes clear that
the basic lesson is a very simple one: trust to nothing and to no one.
Scandal has been betrayed by Mrs Foresight, Prue by Tattle, Ben by
Frail, and Frail and Tattle in their turn by Jeremy (though this is
excusable insofar as they were led to believe, and could hardly have
been expected to doubt, that Jeremy was betraying Valentine). Other
characters betrayed by trust are Foresight in believing in the fidelity
of his wife; Sir Sampson by listening to the blandishments of Angelica;
and Valentine by a misguided faith in his father's humanity. There is
hardly a character in the play who does not at one point trust and who
is not at another point deceived.

   To express the theme of the play in these terms is to make it sound
a rather depressing affair. In fact, as I hope has been evident from
what has been said and quoted already, nothing could be further from
the truth, and it will be necessary to ask why this should be so. The
strange fact is that to live in this world of deceit, treachery, and
compulsive dissimulation is really a rather enjoyable business. The
song called for by Valentine in Act IV expresses the limitations of
such an existence with admirable definiteness, but is equally definite
about the fascination it has for those who have accepted these limitations:

> I tell thee, *Charmion*, could I Time retrieve,
> And could again begin to Love and Live,
> To you I should my earliest Off'ring give;
>   I know my Eyes would lead my Heart to you,
>   And I should all my Vows and Oaths renew,
>   But to be plain, I never would be true.

2

For by our weak and weary Truth, I find,
Love hates to center in a Point assign'd,
But runs with Joy the Circle of the Mind.
Then never let us chain what should be free,
But for relief of either Sex agree,
Since Women love to change, and so do we.

[IV.i.652–64]

Earlier we saw Prue receiving her instruction in the first principles of the game and it was clear that for her, at least at that stage, it was an entirely pleasant game. Tattle and Frail reveal a similar delight in the exercise of their mastery in dissimulation and an even greater delight in making this mastery apparent, in due course, to the victims. When they find themselves deceived in turn, they do not waste words but switch at once and with obvious gusto to trying their skills on each other. Scandal, although admittedly a habitual complainer, is not depressed or horrified by the consummate hypocrisy of Mrs. Foresight—rather the reverse. He is excited by his discovery as a herpetologist might be by that of some new and venomous adder: she is a prodigy of nature and to be revered as such. Whatever we may feel as outsiders about the world of *Love for Love*, we can hardly deny that its inhabitants are thoroughly satisfied at being part of it. Since these inhabitants include Valentine, and seeing that Valentine gives every appearance of sharing the general satisfaction, the task which falls to Angelica of educating him towards higher notions of civility, courtship and herself is to be a much more testing one than those allotted to Frail and Tattle.

II

The climax of *Love for Love* is Angelica's acceptance of the reformed Valentine. It comes in two words, 'Generous *Valentine*', which, although they were written for the mouth of Anne Bracegirdle, not Elizabeth Barry, call for all the eloquence of an 'Ah! poor *Castalio*!' 'Generous' here is a Virgilian characteristic epithet expressing to us the significant truth of Valentine, his singularity and distinction as a human being. It is also, as the concluding point of his education, our chief clue to what the substance of that education has been. The meaning of the word in the seventeenth century was more complex

than its normal sense in modern English would suggest,[2] but seeing
Angelica's words were prompted by the speech of Valentine immedi-
ately preceding them, we can assume that it is here that the nature of
Valentine's generosity will be most clearly displayed:

> *Valentine.* I have been disappointed of my only Hope; and he
> that loses hope may part with any thing. I never valu'd
> Fortune, but as it was subservient to my Pleasure; and my
> only Pleasure was to please this Lady: I have made many
> vain Attempts, and find at last, that nothing but my Ruine
> can effect it: Which, for that Reason, I will sign to——
> Give me the Paper.
>
> [V.i.543–9]

The basic thing is that Valentine has learned to trust and to give,
absolutely and without reservation. When Angelica sees this she is
prepared to give herself just as unconditionally in return. But for her
to have done so without this assurance would have been disastrous. It
is therefore Valentine who has taken the crucial step in resolving the
relationship, and he has done this by challenging the first principle
of town morality on a scale that even the trusting Ben and pliable
Prue might have baulked at.

When we first see Valentine in Act I he is in every sense a creature
of the town. He has exhausted his money in his pursuit of Angelica
(the interpretation of the other characters would be no doubt that
she has milked him of it) but without securing any profession of love
in return. This is hardly surprising: his extravagant spending has been
an attempt to buy her and she has been perfectly aware of this and is
not prepared to be for sale. His next plan, and one that is open to
much the same objections, is to shame her:

> *Valentine.* Well; and now I am poor, I have an opportunity to
> be reveng'd on 'em all; I'll pursue *Angelica* with more Love
> than ever, and appear more notoriously her Admirer in
> this Restraint, than when I openly rival'd the rich Fops,
> that made Court to her; so shall my Poverty be a Mortifi-
> cation to her Pride, . . .
>
> [I.i.49–54]

---

[2] For further discussion of this point see Ben Ross Schneider, *The Ethos of
Restoration Comedy* (Urbana, 1971), pp. 21–36.

Valentine is still in this speech picturing Angelica as a quarry to be hunted, not as a human equal to be loved. It is also clear that his courtship is not directed at her alone, but is simultaneously a performance put on to gain the approbation of the town. In compensation for these imperceptive and rather narcissistic attitudes, we are also made aware of an agreeable impulsiveness, a determination to make the best of whatever his situation offers, and a general openness to new possibilities, which raise him well above the usual pitch of the town. (Being unable to afford breakfast he has been edifying himself with a study of the Stoics.) He still has a chance to change. A visit from the nurse of one of his illegitimate children gives him a chance to display generosity in the limited modern sense by somehow finding her some money and his residual ill-nature by a quip about infanticide. The next visitors are Trapland, a creditor, accompanied by two officers, and, on another errand, Valentine's father's steward. Between them the choice is put to Valentine of accepting his father's proposal for the payment of his debts, which is to surrender his right in the family inheritance, or to go to prison. Valentine consents, as the arrangement will also permit him to leave his lodgings and go in search of Angelica, although here Scandal is pessimistic about his chances:

> *Scandal.* A very desperate demonstration of your love to *Angelica*: And I think she has never given you any assurance of hers.
> *Valentine.* You know her temper; she never gave me any great reason either for hope or despair.
> *Scandal.* Women of her airy temper, as they seldom think before they act, so they rarely give us any light to guess at what they mean: But you have little reason to believe that a Woman of this Age, who has had an indifference for you in your Prosperity, will fall in love with your ill Fortune; besides, *Angelica* has a great Fortune of her own; and great Fortunes either expect another great Fortune, or a Fool.
> [I.i.343–54]

From the town's point of view his reasoning could hardly be faulted.

In the following act we receive our first sight of Angelica and are given no reason to question Scandal's diagnosis of her 'airy temper'. She comes in to demand her uncle's coach, ridicules his harmless obsession with astrology, taunts him openly with his wife's infidelity, confesses to spying on him through a keyhole, and threatens to denounce him to the magistrates as a wizard. None of this is at all serious, but there is still a strong air of gratuitous bullying about it. Our hero has not given very many signs of promise, and neither at this stage does our heroine. Valentine is a town rake and she, to all appearances, is little better than a town miss, superbly adroit in the skills of social manipulation, and not above keeping these skills razor-sharp by a little practice in the domestic circle. What is not clear is whether the purpose of this formidable conversational armoury is offensive or defensive, whether there is an Araminta behind the mask or just another Belinda.

When we see Angelica next she is together for the first time in the play with Valentine and once again she is giving nothing away:

> *Angelica.* You can't accuse me of Inconstancy; I never told you, that I lov'd you.
> *Valentine.* But I can accuse you of Uncertainty, for not telling me whether you did or no.
> *Angelica.* You mistake Indifference for Uncertainty; I never had Concern enough to ask my self the Question.
>
> [III.i.27–32]

Later in the play, at the moment of self-revelation in Act V, we are to discover that she did love him after all; but in the present scene there is no sign of this. And it is not hard to fathom the reasons for Angelica's wariness. Living in a world of Tattles and Frails, she has had to learn to handle their weapons even better than they do themselves. To be in love is to be in a position of vulnerability. The rule of the town is to take advantage of the vulnerable. To be in love, and to reveal this love, is to invite the person you love to take advantage of you. The only safe course, therefore, is to conceal love under the affectation of indifference or dislike. This was Tattle's first lesson to Prue, and an identical principle guides Angelica's behaviour towards Valentine. The problem with Valentine is not simply that he is a town rake and lives by the assumptions of a town rake: that love is a hunt or pursuit, that women are mercenary simpletons to be bought or tricked into submission, that 'He alone won't Betray in whom none will Confide/And the Nymph may be Chaste that has never been Try'd'. If that were all that there was to him, Angelica would not have fallen in love with him in the first place. Valentine in fact has a number of very good and un-town-like instincts. He is not, for instance, interested in money for its own sake but only as a means of helping him to Angelica. (Though this still, of course, makes him guilty of the assumption that she is available to be bought.) His real trouble is that he insists on interpreting other people's behaviour, including Angelica's, according to the cynical principles of the town and Scandal. He is therefore in the grip of two wrong images, one of himself and one of Angelica, each reinforcing the other. For Angelica to reveal the wrongness of his image of her, which would not be hard as it is largely of her own creation, would be of no use until he had learned to interpret such an action according to principles other than those of the Age. It is only when he has made the break-through of his own accord and come to see himself in completely new terms that it will be safe for her to reveal that she is not what he thought she was. It is this which Angelica is trying to explain to him when at the end of the scene he asks her whether she is going to 'come to a Resolution' and she replies 'I can't. Resolution must come to me, or I shall never have one.' It is Valentine who has to find both their ways out of the vicious circle.

At this stage in the play, however, the probability of such a break-through does not seem very high. The immediate task of Scandal and Valentine is to test the genuineness of Angelica's indifference, with the aim, should they find any evidence of feigning, of exploiting the revealed vulnerability as ruthlessly as possible. Scandal, whose power to fathom the masks and stratagems of the town has already been presented for our admiration in Act I, is clearly of the opinion that there is more to her behaviour than meets the eye. Taking up her 'I never had Concern enough to ask my self the Question' quoted earlier, he inserts a sly hint of his disbelief:

> *Scandal.* Nor good Nature enough to answer him that did ask you: I'll say that for you, Madam.
> *Angelica.* What, are you setting up for good Nature?
> *Scandal.* Only for the affectation of it, as the Women do for ill Nature.
>
> [III.i.33–7]

Scandal's insight here amounts to nothing more than the normal town assumption that things are probably the reverse of what they seem, or, as Tattle enlarges, 'All well-bred Persons Lie! . . . you must never speak what you think: Your words must contradict your thoughts. . . .' In reply to this, Angelica is rather surprisingly prepared to concede that he may be right but challenges him to persuade

Valentine of this. For Angelica knows that Valentine has no real understanding of her and to this extent cannot seriously threaten her. And Valentine, again rather surprisingly, is perfectly prepared to confess to his ignorance both of her and mankind: 'I shall receive no Benefit from the Opinion: For I know no effectual Difference between continued Affectation and Reality.' This passage is sometimes quoted out of context as if it were a statement of Congreve's personal attitude towards social role-playing, but this is not so. The point of the lines is to show the inadequacy of Valentine's understanding both of himself and of others, for there *is* a difference between reality and continued affectation, a difference which Angelica understands perfectly because it is something she has to live with all the time.

The same issues, along with one or two new ones, inform the comedy of the subsequent scene between Angelica, the two men, and Tattle. Tattle embodies the values and expectations of the town in their purest state. Where Valentine had felt unable to distinguish between continued affectation and reality but was not prepared to deny that there was such a difference, Tattle is so far gone as to have mistaken his own affectations for reality. His conversation is a long romance on the theme of his prowess as a lover. At the same time, as we saw in Act I, he is inordinately proud of his reputation for discretion. This is partly an effect of his desire to be thought a wit and partly a technique of seduction in its own right, on the principle that women would be more inclined to have affairs with a man who could be relied on to keep it a secret. At the present juncture he is exhibiting his accomplishments, secrecy among them, for the benefit of Angelica. The fun of the scene lies in the careful manœuvring by which Valentine and Scandal set his two reputations at odds with each other, a subtle exercise in the art which Wilkinson calls 'enjoying the fool'.[3] In trying to defend his reputation for secrecy he is forced to assert that he had 'never had the good Fortune to be trusted once with a Lady's Secret'. This brings the objection from Angelica 'But whence comes the Reputation of Mr. *Tattle*'s Secresie, if he was never trusted?', putting him in the position of having to betray his reputation in order to defend it:

> *Tattle.* Well, my Witnesses are not present——But I
> confess I have had Favours from Persons——But as the
> Favours are numberless, so the Persons are nameless.
> *Scandal.* Pooh, pox, this proves nothing.

<hr>

3 *The Comedy of Habit*, p. 84.

Tattle. No? I can shew Letters, Locketts, Pictures, and Rings, and if there be occasion for Witnesses, I can summon the Maids at the Chocolate-Houses, all the Porters of *Pall-Mall* and *Covent-Garden*, the Door-keepers at the Play-House, the Drawers at *Locket's*, *Pontack's*, the *Rummer*, *Spring Garden*; my own Landlady and *Valet de Chambre*; all who shall make Oath, that I receive more Letters than the Secretary's Office; and that I have more Vizor-Masks to enquire for me, than ever went to see the Hermaphrodite, or the Naked Prince. And it is notorious, that in a Country Church, once, an Enquiry being made, who I was, it was answer'd, I was the famous *Tattle*, who had ruin'd so many Women.

Valentine. It was there, I suppose, you got the Nick-Name of the *Great Turk*.

Tattle. True; I was call'd *Turk-Tattle* all over the Parish———

[III.i.149–68]

Tattle's narcissistic male egotism is exactly what Angelica is trying to protect herself from. However, his situation is also relevant to hers in another way. As he has destroyed his reputation for secrecy in defending it; so she is still in the position where to reveal her love to an unregenerate Valentine would be to resign herself for ever to the role of conquered quarry. Hers is a genuine secrecy, unlike Tattle's fraudulent one, but is just as self-defeating.

By this time Scandal has a strong suspicion that Angelica is more kindly disposed than she would have the men believe. When he exits it is with the promise to Valentine 'I've something in my Head to communicate to you'—presumably the pretence of madness which is to be Valentine's last and most daring throw in his attempt to confound his father and to extract a capitulation from Angelica on his terms rather than hers. Angelica is the first to call on him after his supposed condition has been proclaimed, and on her entrance comes close to betraying her real feelings. 'She's concern'd, and loves him' is Scandal's diagnosis. But Scandal has forgotten, or perhaps never realized, that she is quite as brilliant a penetrator of pretence as himself, and he betrays his own game by an unguarded wink to Jeremy. Having gauged the true situation, Angelica's responsibility is to repay trick with trick, which she does by denying outright that she loves Valentine and then announcing on the basis of excellent London reasons that she will not see him after all:

> But I have consider'd that Passions are unreasonable
> and involuntary; if he loves, he can't help it; and if I don't
> love, I can't help it; no more than he can help his being a
> Man, or I my being a Woman; or no more than I can help
> my want of Inclination to stay longer here . . .
>
> [IV.i.86–90]

Angelica here is doing no more than give the men the treatment
appropriate to the role in which they insist on casting her. She sweeps
out leaving Scandal undisturbed in his belief in the weathercock
nature of 'this same Womankind'. Later she will be back to put
Valentine through his paces more thoroughly.

Angelica resents the situation because it shows that Valentine is
still seeing the world in terms of Scandal's bitter satiric vignettes at
the close of Act I, among them 'Pride, Folly, Affectation, Wantonness,
Inconstancy, Covetousness, Dissimulation, Malice, and Ignorance' as
the image of a 'celebrated Beauty'. But it is now Valentine's turn to
grow satirical: his 'madness' takes the form of ringing denunciations
directed at such targets as lawyers, citizens, and elderly husbands;
when he comes to address Angelica, however, the tone changes and
the accents of simulated madness give way to a perfectly composed
beauty:

> *Angelica.* Do you know me, *Valentine?*
> *Valentine.* Oh very well.
> *Angelica.* Who am I?
> *Valentine.* You're a Woman,———One to whom Heav'n
> gave Beauty, when it grafted Roses on a Briar. You are
> the reflection of Heav'n in a Pond, and he that leaps at
> you is sunk. You are all white, a sheet of lovely spotless
> Paper, when you first are Born; but you are to be scrawl'd
> and blotted by every Goose's Quill. I know you; for I
> lov'd a Woman, and lov'd her so long, that I found out a
> strange thing: I found out what a Woman was good for.
> *Tattle.* Aye, prithee, what's that?
> *Valentine.* Why to keep a Secret.
> *Tattle.* O Lord!
> *Valentine.* O exceeding good to keep a Secret: For tho' she
> should tell, yet she is not to be believ'd.
>
> [IV.i.631–46]

The speech is one of the few in the play where Congreve's language
achieves a genuine richness of poetic implication, yet once again the

images are expressions of an imperfect understanding: Angelica had asked Valentine if he knew her, and he reveals very clearly in his reply that he knows only the false self she shows to the town. He does not see that the scrawls and blots are of his own imagination: that were he to leap, he would not be sunk at all. Yet the closing lines do suggest that he has intimations of a truth unknown to him before the experiment with madness. Angelica has indeed kept a secret, two secrets in fact: that she is in love with him, and that she is not the person he and the town take her for. He is beginning to know this without knowing that he knows.

There is still, however, a long way to go. Angelica is not yet won; she is still resentful of the contemptuous shallowness of his artifices; and when he trustingly confesses the stratagem, she will not yield an inch in return. His request is that, as he puts off his pretence of madness, so she should suspend her affectation of disregard:

> Nay faith, now let us understand one another,
> Hypocrisie apart,———The Comedy draws toward an
> end, and let us think of leaving acting, and be our selves;
> and since you have lov'd me, you must own I have at
> length deserv'd you shou'd confess it.
>
> [IV.i.706–10]

This is too simple altogether. For one thing it shows that he still regards courtship as a matter of trickery and charades. So Angelica repays him in kind by pretending that she still believes him to be mad and treating his protestations of sanity as a madman's self-delusion. She is also quick to take him up on his reasons for adopting the stratagem:

Valentine. . . . my seeming
Madness has deceiv'd my Father, and procur'd me time to think of means to reconcile me to him; and preserve the right of my Inheritance to his Estate; which otherwise by Articles, I must this Morning have resign'd: And this I had inform'd you of to Day, but you were gone, before I knew you had been here.

Angelica. How! I thought your love of me had caus'd this Transport in your Soul; which, it seems, you only counterfeited, for mercenary Ends and sordid Interest.

Valentine. Nay, now you do me Wrong; for if any Interest was considered, it was yours; since I thought I wanted

more than Love, to make me worthy of you.
Angelica. Then you thought me mercenary———But how
   am I deluded by this Interval of Sense, to reason with a
   Madman?

[IV.i.715–30]

Valentine's frankness has been returned with a town miss's trick which,
of course, he knows to be a town miss's trick. But he is also to be
given a clue to the secret which still eludes him. Before she leaves,
Angelica speaks to him in words which have some of the elegiac
quality of his own mad language, and which are her most explicit
statement of her sense of the situation:

Valentine. You are not leaving me in this Uncertainty?
Angelica. Wou'd any thing, but a Madman complain of
   Uncertainty? Uncertainty and Expectation are the Joys of
   Life. Security is an insipid thing, and the overtaking and
   possessing of a Wish, discovers the Folly of the Chase.
   Never let us know one another better; for the Pleasure of
   a Masquerade is done, when we come to shew Faces;
   But I'll tell you two things before I leave you; I am not
   the Fool you take me for; and you are Mad and don't
   know it.

[ll. 784–93]

In returning him the unmasking image Angelica is conceding what is
after all a central fact of the play—that the world of masks, of illusion,
of inconstancy, of trickery, of unceasing psychological combat, of
the rake's pursuit and the woman's hypocritical refusal, the world in
which 'Love hates to center in a Point assign'd,/But runs with Joy
the Circle of the Mind', is in its way an exciting, testing world.
Valentine has thoroughly enjoyed his life in it, and so far he has
resisted all her attempts to make him leave it. But now that Angelica
has seen beyond it she is not to be drawn back. For all its dazzle
and movement it is a world in which it is impossible to trust or to
love. The relationship of Angelica and Valentine has been conducted
along the lines prescribed by the world and behind the masks of its
making. When Valentine asks her to take off her mask it is in the
expectation of finding a face beneath which will be not very different
from the mask. Appreciating this, Angelica is only being fair in
warning him that 'the Pleasure of a Masquerade is done, when we
come to shew Faces'. If they were to live their lives according to the

town's terms there would always have to be some kind of mask in place. But what if the face beneath the mask were itself a mask and the face beneath that second mask one that Valentine had never dreamed of? If this were so it is possible that she might after all not be a fool, which is the rake's basic assumption about the women he pursues by trick and bribe, and that Valentine might well be led into actions which by all the standards of the town (and when the moment comes Scandal is to use exactly this word) are 'mad' ones. If she does not succeed in enlightening him she is at least able to puzzle him. 'She is harder to be understood than a Piece of *Ægyptian* Antiquity, or an *Irish* Manuscript; you may pore till you spoil your Eyes, and not improve your Knowledge' [ll. 801-4]. Yet he has at least recognized that there is a mystery and that his 'Lesson' must have a 'Moral'; which is a start. And at the close of the scene he is even prepared to query one of the dicta of the hitherto infallible Scandal.

By the time we see him again he has discovered the answer which, all things considered, is a very simple one. For Scandal's principle of 'trust to no one' he has substituted another—'if you do trust, trust absolutely'—and his trust is rewarded. At the very moment he is about to give assent to the deed of disinheritance, Angelica tears the earlier bond and in the same breath renounces the marriage with Sir Sampson. What is it that he has discovered to bring about this change? His preparedness to sacrifice himself is the most obvious thing; but this is itself the fruit of a deeper awareness. The solution is in her answer to the question he asks her before he proceeds to sign to his own undoing:

'Tis true, you have a great while pretended Love
to me; nay, what if you were sincere? still you must
pardon me, if I think my own Inclinations have a better
Right to dispose of my Person, than yours.

[V.i.531-4]

The notion that other people's persons should be in their own disposal, and not one's own, is not particularly original, but the difficulty that Valentine has had in reaching it should caution us against imagining it to be self-evident. For the whole system of the town had been built on an explicit denial of it. Valentine has at last emerged from the delusion, and through this from his poverty. Ironically enough the second part of the benison has been brought about by the most arrant town trick of all—and its perpetrator has been Angelica.

III

We have followed the action of *Love for Love* through to the point of resolution. The question still has to be asked whether that resolution is a satisfactory one. Triviality and self-seeking are to be countered with idealism; but how valid is the countering? May it not be open to the accusation of sentimental unreality just as Congreve's presentation of the world may be to the charge of immature cynicism? Both these suggestions have been made.

Part of the trouble here lies in the abstract, externalized way in which Congreve presents his resolution. Assuming that the real climax of the play is Valentine's acceptance of Angelica not as a quarry or an opponent but as a fellow human being with exactly the same rights as himself, it can still be argued that we do not actually experience what this realization means for Valentine. The crucial stage in his growth to realization comes between his exit in Act IV and his entrance in Act V. By the time he reappears he has discovered what previously eluded him; but we are not shown how this happens or what it feels like to have it happen; we simply have to accept it as it is stated. The same holds for Angelica. The assumption of the play is that behind the façade of the town jilt there is a profound longing for those human satisfactions that the town ignores and a genuine capacity for unselfish love; but it is only in isolated speeches that we have any direct sense of this part of her; the rest has to be deduced from things that she states in a fairly abstract way and the nature of her reactions to the stratagems of Valentine and Scandal.

I would suggest that this effect was quite deliberate on Congreve's part and is an important clue to the kind of comedy he is writing. Here we need to remember that the immediate ancestor of Restoration comedy is not Jacobean comedy but that phase of Caroline comedy when it was most under the influence of the court masque. The essence of a masque, to borrow a phrase from Chapter I, is that it should give 'sensuous life to abstract formulations'. In comedy under the influence of the masque the playwright's primary interest will be the profile of the idea rather than depth of characterization and we should not complain if the persons of the drama are occasionally allowed to dwindle into cut-outs. One could argue that this kind of comedy is more restricted in its possibilities than the kind which takes personality as its starting point and allows us not only to observe the actions of the characters, but to share in their inner growth;

yet having conceded this, one is not entitled to judge one kind as if it were an unsuccessful attempt at the other. (If we object to Congreve's methods we should remember that they are also Molière's and Shaw's.) The minuet of ideas which is the structural basis of Congreve's play is there to be appreciated as a minuet, the theatrical articulation of an abstract ideal of love and gentility. Congreve is not particularly interested in how these ideals are to be made workable at the level of individual, everyday living, or at least not in *Love for Love*.

For these reasons, the criticism of the play which claims that its values are arbitrary and unrealized seems to me a little beside the point. There is still, moreover, the question of whether the abstract ideals so elegantly traced out in the course of the minuet are the true informing values of the comedy. I would suggest that they are probably not, and that the most valuable thing the play has to give us is much simpler. Despite its preoccupation with the least sublime of human passions, its singularly unsatisfactory gallery of characters, and Congreve's insistence on showing us just why these characters are unsatisfactory, the overall sense given by *Love for Love* is of an immense and heartening liveliness—one is tempted to say a joy. Squalid and selfish as the creatures of the town are, they do not repel us in the way the corresponding characters in Jonson do and we may even envy them their unconquerable bravura and their outrageous and wholly unjustified self-admiration, much as on a larger scale we do Falstaff's. I suggested earlier that *Love for Love* was the most Shakespearean of Congreve's plays. In an influential essay contrasting the Shakespearean and Jonsonian styles in comedy Nevill Coghill suggested that the essence of the former lay in the assertion 'that life is to be grasped'.[4] This is surely the reason why Congreve's characters remain attractive. Despite the fact that the life they possess is by any objective standard paltry, dishonest, and trivial, they are prepared to lay hold of it with every atom of energy in their beings. There can be a vividness, an elevation, even to being a fop, a tyrannical braggart, or a temporarily stranded porpoise, as long as one is prepared to take possession of the role with the self-proclaiming gusto of a Tattle, a Sampson, or a Ben. There may even be a sublimity of sorts in being a cuckold philosopher if one can say with the heroic fatalism of Foresight, 'Why if I was born to be a Cuckold, there's no more to be said—.' In the case of Valentine the spectacle is one of a character who

[4] Nevill Coghill, 'The Basis of Shakespearean Comedy' in Anne Ridler ed., *Shakespeare Criticism 1935–1960* (London, 1970), p. 203.

has succeeded in extracting 'a quintessence even from nothingness'—understanding from madness, truth from jest, love from despair, generosity from selfishness. It is our sense of this miracle, this heroic laying hold of every possibility of even the most tawdry and unsatisfactory existence which allows us to claim for *Love for Love* a rank among Restoration comedies only just beneath that of *The Way of the World*.

5

The Way of the World

I

Love for Love is certainly Congreve's most infectiously enjoyable play, yet it is to *The Way of the World* that his admirers and his detractors have both agreed to look for the true measure of his stature as a dramatist. Lytton Strachey called it 'among the most wonderful and glorious creations of the human mind'.[1] No one else has ever quite risen to this level of enthusiasm and a number of critics have dissented sharply, but even to concede that the judgement was not wholly irresponsible would still be to rate the comedy very highly indeed. Certainly, it is the play in which Congreve comes closest to challenging Jonson for the position of our most important classical writer of comedy after Shakespeare, and if in the event few of us would be prepared to adjudicate in its favour against *The Alchemist*, *Volpone* or *Bartholmew Fair*, it is a much better comedy than Jonson, or perhaps any other dramatist, had written by the age of thirty.

The social arena of *The Way of the World* is basically that of *Love for Love*. Lady Wishfort is the widow of one country knight and plans remarriage with another. Her nephew, Sir Willfull Witwoud, has his seat in Shropshire. However, Lady Wishfort has abandoned the country for the town bringing with her her daughter Arabella whose history prior to the play has been firstly a marriage to a Mr. Languish of unknown status and origin but presumably rich, next a widowhood enlivened by an affair with Edward Mirabell, and finally a hasty

[1] *Portraits in Miniature and Other Essays* (London, 1931), p. 49, quoted by Norman N. Holland, *The First Modern Comedies* (Cambridge, U.S.A., 1959), p. 175.

marriage, under the mistaken impression that she is pregnant by Mirabell, to the unsuspecting Fainall. Another refugee from the shires is Sir Willfull's half brother Anthony Witwoud who, having escaped the threat of being bound apprentice to a maker of felts in Shrewsbury by becoming a student of Old Pumplenose the attorney at Furnival's Inn, has now graduated to town fop and coffee-house exquisite. The other characters are not identified specifically with the country and may be presumed to belong to the town, Millamant and Mirabell representing the highest level of its accomplishments, Fainall and Marwood a lower and uglier, but still considerable one, and Petulant a lower still. The crucial issue is that all the major characters except Fainall and the two fops seem to have possession in their own right of inherited wealth. Fainall has enriched himself through his marriage to Arabella and by pillaging Marwood, but is now deeply in debt and with no prospect of obtaining further funds except by extending his depredations to his mother-in-law. He is a self-proclaimed fortune-hunter, and is not treated by the others as a person of any particular consequence except in his power to hurt. There is a suggestion of obscure origins and even of the class enemy about him though this does not have the significance it had with Maskwell in *The Double Dealer*. The social allegiances which dominate the play are therefore those of the upper level of the country gentry and their town relations.

The play is also, as were its two predecessors, concerned with the fortunes of a family and, like *The Double Dealer*, but unlike *Love for Love*, is interested in the family as a family, not just as a collection of individuals. The family concerned is that whose founder was Lady Wishfort's father. He also had two other daughters, one of whom was the mother of Millamant (I assume this is a surname) and the other of Sir Wilfull Witwoud. Anthony Witwoud is the son of Sir Wilfull's father by a second marriage. Fainall has become a member of the family by marrying Arabella Languish and Mirabell will do the same when he marries Millamant. Moreover it is clear that the direction of dynastic growth for the future will be through Mirabell and Millamant and the son who is promised to us in the famous 'proviso' scene. Mrs. Fainall in the course of two marriages and at least one affair has so far failed to produce children, and Sir Wilfull has 'no mind to marry'. Thus the marriage towards which the play moves will have some of the dynastic significance of that of Cynthia and Mellefont in *The Double Dealer*.

The emphasis given by Congreve to kin relationships leads to the same kinds of conflict between what Norman Holland has distinguished as 'emotional' and 'dynastic' realities that we have already seen in *The Double Dealer*.[2] In an ideal world, kin relationships and personal affinities would coincide. Children would love their parents, and husbands their wives. The family would be a completely stable organism. In *The Way of the World* it is almost true to say that the reverse is the case. Fainall and Mrs. Fainall detest each other utterly. Lady Wishfort is at odds with her niece Millamant. Witwoud has nothing but contempt for the country ways of his brother. There is also the complication of Mrs. Fainall's previous relationship with Mirabell, though this does not seem to interfere with her friendship with Millamant, or her co-operation in their schemes against Lady Wishfort. Lady Wishfort is herself in love with Mirabell and endeavours to obtain revenge on him by marrying his supposed uncle, Sir Rowland, who is actually Mirabell's servant Waitwell in disguise. One of Mirabell's main problems is how to bring these personal affinities and antipathies into some kind of harmony with the formal obligations of kinship. If he cannot accomplish this the family will simply crumble to pieces at the first assault from outside. To make matters even more difficult, there is still another complicating factor to be kept in mind, namely the law. As well as dealing to the best of their abilities with conflicts of love and obligation, the characters also have to act in accordance with legal constraints expressed in wills, deeds, entails and marriage settlements. Through one of these Lady Wishfort has gained control over part of Millamant's inheritance. Through another, Fainall thinks he has control of his wife's money. Through yet another, Mirabell possesses the whole of Mrs. Fainall's estate in trust thus negating Fainall's document. Mirabell also refers in Act V to a contract 'in Writing' between himself and Millamant. Finally there is Sir Rowland's 'black box', which Lady Wishfort believes gives him the power to reduce Mirabell to poverty.

In coming to *The Way of the World* from *Love for Love* one is conscious of a definite darkening of tone. *Love for Love* is a play of triumphant vitality in whose world villainy, despite its extravagant assertions to the contrary, is totally without menace. In *The Way of the World* villainy is no longer a purely comic spectacle: its power is real and immediate. At the same time there is nothing of the sublime self-satisfaction that is the privilege of even the defeated characters in

[2] Holland, op. cit., p. 178.

Love for Love. Fainall would like to be a Mirabell, Marwood a Millamant. Lady Wishfort is in despairing flight from the realization that
she is old and ugly. It is in each of these respects a much less comforting
play than *Love for Love*: its main dramatic emphasis is on how people
interact in a world which is a recognizable simulacrum of the real
one and in which life choices are to be measured by the canons that
apply in the real one. Although things turn out right in the end, we
recognize that under slightly altered circumstances, and given a less
formidable champion than Mirabell, they could quite conceivably have
turned out wrong.

To re-apply the terms used in the previous chapter, we might say
that in this play Congreve has moved away from a Shakespearian-
festive towards a Jonsonian-corrective view of comedy. The particular
society he is concerned with is, as we have seen already, a selfish,
combative one, in which personal survival is dependent on skill in
deception, and in which one's status is ultimately a matter of how
adept one is in enlisting other people's energies in the cause of one's
own advancement. It is the Hobbesian world of self-seeking writ
small in Covent Garden, and where the absolute authority of a Mirabell
must be accepted before men and women will agree to live at peace
with each other. In *The Old Batchelour* Congreve had looked with
amused detachment at the way people interacted in this world,
articulating the patterns of manipulation and counter-manipulation
which underlie the elegant exchanges, with the persuasive accuracy
of a seventeenth century Erving Goffman. In *The Way of the World*,
although a good deal of the detachment and some of the amusement
have gone, the basic interest remains the same. The central conflict
is one between two arch-manipulators, Mirabell and Fainall, the
issue between them being the rather squalid one of which is to have
an old woman's money. Although Mirabell is clearly on the side of
right and Fainall on that of wrong, their methods are virtually identical.
Of course, we do not see the affair in quite as bleak a light as this would
imply insofar as manipulation in this sense may be practised with
considerable grace and polish, and in a spirit bordering on the aesthetic.
(This, at any rate, seems to be the only excuse for Mirabell's needlessly
over-elaborate 'Sir Rowland' stratagem.) Nonetheless, if the deception
fails and the mask falls, the face beneath can be an ugly one. This is
certainly so of Marwood and Fainall, the losers, but it could equally
well have been Mirabell's case had he not been so splendidly the
winner. The only thing that can be unequivocally advanced as evi-

dence for his moral probity is that although possessed through a
deed of trust of Mrs. Fainall's money he did not attempt, as he easily
might, to cheat her of it, and indeed for the world whose ways we are
asked to inspect, this is the height of practicable virtue—anything
beyond would be folly and cast doubt upon the possessor's ability
to survive. The general point here is that the norms against which
we measure human conduct in *The Way of the World* are fairly low
ones, and that looked at narrowly (though in a way in which the
play does not particularly encourage us to look) the equipment of
the hero would be seen to include quite a number of items which
might more appropriately have been reserved for the villain. In this
the play is pointing to the truth that received its classical enunciation
fourteen years later from Bernard Mandeville: that it is not only the
'desire of Company, good Nature, Pity, Affability, and other Graces
of a fair Outside' which make man a sociable animal, but that 'his
vilest and most hateful Qualities are the most necessary Accomplishments to fit him for the largest and according to the World, the
happiest and most flourishing Societies'.[3]

II

The basic fact of social life is therefore manipulation, and the two
arch-manipulators are Mirabell and Fainall. (Millamant may have a
claim to even higher regard but is content for the most part to let
Mirabell act on her behalf.) Of the two it is Fainall who has the
advantage of the most clearly defined objectives: he needs money
and he hates his wife, something which is hardly surprising when we
consider that his declared aim in marrying was 'to make lawful
Prize of a rich Widow's Wealth' [II.i.206–7]. We may also suspect a
disinterested hatred for the family which has used him, though he
does not as yet fully realize the fact, quite as ruthlessly as he intends
to use it. A problem of a lesser order is presented by his affair with
Mrs. Marwood. He is cooling, but having spent her money and
being under threat of exposure to his wife is forced to feign continued
interest. (The excellent National Theatre production of 1969–70
caught this beautifully by having the two undress for each other with
expressions of profound ennui.) His main design, which slowly
ripens during the first three acts, and, with the aid of inside knowledge

[3] Bernard Mandeville, *The Fable of the Bees*, ed. Phillip Harth (Harmondsworth, 1970), p. 53.

Gc

fortuitously acquired by Marwood, is sprung in the fourth, is to gain an ascendancy over his wife which will permit him to live apart from her, and at the same time give him power over the remainder of her portion, along with what is yet to come to her from her mother. Lady Wishfort, to complicate the matter further, still has custody of over half of Millamant's inheritance, which will become her own if Millamant marries against her wishes; Fainall would not mind having that as well. As the action proceeds an additional motive gains ground, that of revenge on Mirabell. At the beginning of the play, Fainall has become aware that Marwood is attracted to Mirabell; later comes the revelation that his marriage was arranged by Mirabell and that his wife had been Mirabell's mistress. (This is the one moment of the play where, perhaps, we sympathize with him.) But the news brings its own compensation in that it is exactly the weapon he needs to get control of her money.

Fainall's position of power arises from the disparities outlined earlier that exist in the world of the play between familial obligation, personal affinity and legal compulsion, and which are the main reason for the frantic prodigies of dissimulation which are the normal way of life for most of its people. One is likely at any time to find oneself under the necessity of reconciling irreconcilables. In Mrs. Fainall's case, for instance, there is duty to a mother, affection for a lover whose aim is to cheat and humiliate that mother, and the need to keep up appearances with a husband for whom she has nothing but contempt. Over and above this there is the fundamental imperative of maintaining the honour and prestige of her family. Fainall, as a fortune hunter, has no family; he has simply become a supernumerary member of his wife's. Her infidelity, insofar as it is a personal injury, is of no particular use to him; but, as a means of exposing her to public dishonour, it gives him power over the whole body of her relatives, each of whose reputation and prestige would suffer with hers. Fainall's aim, like Maskwell's, is to reconstruct the family so as to put himself at least temporarily at its head. He fails because in the moment of peril the family instinctively gathers around the new protector Mirabell, and because Mrs. Fainall, at the time of her marriage, had secretly transferred her money out of her own hands. Fainall can still damage the family, but only at the expense of impoverishing himself which they know he is not prepared to do. His downfall involves not just the end of his tempting dreams of wealth and independence, but the realization that the rest of his life is to be spent in total subjection to

the family. Thus it is the sword of Sir Wilfull, its senior male representative, which is drawn in Mrs. Fainall's defence at the close of the
play, not, as we might have expected, Mirabell's. But the ultimate
humiliation is not this but the fact that his wife and Mirabell have
beaten him at his own game—manipulation. Every step he took had
been allowed for. Every attempt to use others had brought him closer
to the ultimate folly of total self-revelation.

It is Mirabell then, of the men, who is held up for our admiration
as the most accomplished manipulator; moreover, it is in this talent
that his status as wit-hero lies. In the school of civility, his is to be
the first prize, and this without much benefit from the 'suprasocial'
(Holland's term) insights so painfully acquired by Valentine. Not that
even Mirabell has an entirely clean slate. At the beginning of the play
he has already failed in an attempt to win Millamant by pretending
love to Lady Wishfort. In the opening acts, he is busy, though with
quite what degree of seriousness is not entirely clear, launching the
elaborate scheme in which his valet Waitwell, posing as an uncle
with the power to disinherit him, is to attempt to lure Lady Wishfort
into a sham marriage from which the price of release will be her
acceptance of Mirabell's terms for his marriage with Millamant.
(What Millamant thinks of this plan is not made clear. It hardly seems
her style.) The plot, however, is betrayed before it is even sprung,
and, after being used to extract some readily exploitable fun, is quietly
dropped. The real index of Mirabell's abilities in moving others to
act in accordance with his interests is not found in these elaborate
schemes but in his skill at persuading other characters to assist him
in them. For a start, there is the case of Mrs. Fainall. From being his
mistress, and at one stage we are led to believe she still loves him, she
has come to be his agent in deceiving her mother and bringing about
a marriage between him and her cousin. She does this without any
indication of regret or embarrassment and, although the betrayal
of the scheme is ultimately her fault, there is not the slightest suggestion
of malice or dissimulation on her part. The relationship is a puzzling
one for a modern reader. Is she a female Dorimant patiently waiting
for satiety to bring Mirabell back to her? This can hardly be so, for
everything we are shown of her suggests that she is amiable, well
intentioned, and disinterestedly concerned for the happiness of her
cousin as well as her lover. (And note the delicate moment at IV.i.284
where Millamant before accepting Mirabell in effect asks Fainall's
permission to do so.) sI she worried about the money she had entrusted

to him? He shows at the end of the play that there was no need for
her to have been so, and there is certainly not the slighest hint of this
in the text. There is also the problem of her decision to marry Fainall.
The marriage was arranged by Mirabell and had proved an utter
disaster. 'Why did you make me marry this man?' she asks him, and
the tone of his reply is that of an impatient teacher repeating a simple
and much-rehearsed lesson to a dim-witted child:

> *Mirabell.* Why do we daily commit disagreeable and dan-
> gerous Actions? To save that Idol Reputation. If the
> familiarities of our Loves had produc'd that Consequence,
> of which you were apprehensive, where could you have
> fix'd a Father's Name with Credit, but on a Husband? I
> knew *Fainall* to be a Man lavish of his Morals, an interested
> and professing Friend, a false and a designing Lover; yet
> one whose Wit and outward fair Behaviour have gain'd a
> Reputation with the Town, enough to make that Woman
> stand excus'd, who has suffer'd herself to be won by his
> Addresses. A better Man ought not to have been sacrific'd
> to the Occasion; a worse had not answer'd to the Purpose.
> When you are weary of him, you know your Remedy.
>
> [II.i.265-77]

The attitudes towards love and marriage which lie behind these
remarks are perhaps the hardest things in the play for us to grasp.
They raise all kinds of questions whose answers seem hidden from us
by impenetrable cultural barriers. Why did not Mirabell marry her
himself? If he simply thought she was not worth it why does she
accept this so calmly? Was it that she had had other lovers? Did the
affair come to an end with the marriage or did it continue? Could the
point of the scene be to show Mirabell as a cold hearted Machiavel and
Mrs. Fainall as a gullible simpleton; or is there some unspoken,
inviolable canon known to contemporaries but not to us which
would have justified it? And what is the remedy Mirabell mentions?
Is it simply to reveal her financial independence to her husband? Is
it to take another lover? Is it for Mirabell to pick a quarrel with
Fainall and kill him? All these and many other possibilities present
themselves the moment we try to ask why people should think about
such things in such a way. Even Mrs. Fainall's initial complaint is
ambiguous. Is it being married at all under these circumstances that
she objects to or being married to Fainall in particular? Whatever

the answers—if there ever were answers—it is abundantly clear that, despite the apparent unsatisfactoriness of Mirabell's actions and replies, Mrs. Fainall is still very well disposed towards him, and is prepared to accept his reproof quite as meekly as she has accepted his designs against her mother. This would argue powers of persuasion of no ordinary kind.

So far we have been looking at the theme of manipulation at the larger level of plot and intrigue, but this is by no means the whole story, nor are Mirabell's talents in this field purely a matter of persuasiveness and a gift for coining stratagems. As was the case in *The Old Batchelour*, even the most casual conversational encounter may turn into a joust for dominance, and a number of apparently offhand remarks can be shown to have their component of combativeness or defensiveness. The chief difference from the earlier play is that where the combatants of *The Old Batchelour* favoured the open wit duel, the characters of *The Way of the World*, in that they work from within a more consistent and certainly more elaborate code of civility, have to insinuate their attitudes in much subtler ways than were permitted to Bellmour and Belinda. Each is an adept in the art of gentle lessening and can be shown to be putting that art to work in a number of contexts where the reader of today neither expects it nor is particularly well equipped to recognize it. This is especially so of Mirabell whose position of near total dominance in group encounters is dependent for its continuance on the art with which it is concealed.

One of the problems which the dialogue of *The Way of the World* presents the modern actor and producer is that it is built up out of the language of a society in which politeness, deference and verbal indirection were the norms of everyday discourse, and any direct expression of strong emotion regarded as ill-bred and boorish. This limitation gives rise to a major problem of communication. If one is not permitted to express hostility openly how is one to go about it? One way is to become noticeably more polite than is strictly called for by the situation, an art at which Englishmen of a certain kind are still very adroit. For Congreve's generation it was a new and somewhat stunning discovery. Quite minor alterations to the elaborate formulae of compliment and civility could bear a heavy burden of implication. We are familiar with the refinements of irony practised by Pope and Swift—and Congreve, we should remember, was the friend of both—but literary irony is only a reflection of a much more widely cultivated skill. The interest of the age in various kinds of dissimulated speech is shown by the number of words they had for it: there was 'smoking', 'shamming', 'huffing', 'roasting', 'rallying', 'bantering', 'dumbfounding', and 'quizzing'; one might 'sell someone a bargain' or 'make a bubble' of him. D. R. M. Wilkinson speaks of 'a discipline of suspicion among the gallants' and identifies its prime elements as detraction, dissimulation, and 'the art of inverting'.[4] However, it was not only the men and women of fashion who indulged in this: even the great Dutch scientist Hermann Boerhaave, the last universal mind of Western Europe and the intellectual wonder of the age, was an earnest cultivator of 'that polite kind of irony so much admired by the ancients in Socrates' and in his lectures was able to excite 'laughter in the whole audience without the alteration of one muscle in his own face'.[5] The ability to convey one thing to one hearer and another thing altogether to a second was one of the fundamental skills of group interaction. Congreve constructs whole scenes around this (e.g. Fainall's and Mirabell's quizzing of Witwoud in I.i. and the corresponding scene in I.i. of *Love for Love* between Mellefont, Scandal and Tattle). In reading him we must therefore always be prepared for the possibility that the attitude expressed may not have anything to do with the attitude intended.

This caution is particularly important for the opening scene of *The Way of the World*. Ian Donaldson has claimed that on our first meeting with Fainall and Mirabell it is not possible from their language alone to tell the difference between them.[6] Brian Gibbons on the other hand sees a 'fluidity and uncertainty' about the exchange:

> In the opening dialogue there is a subtle instability of tone; the hints, evasions, and insinuations convey the impression of much being withheld; and precisely this impression is necessary to a proper understanding of the play, which is concerned to bring this intricate texture, the texture of real life in society, into focus with traditional ideals of comedy.[7]

An eighteenth-century audience, I feel, would have agreed with Gibbons rather than Donaldson but have wanted to be much more

[4] *The Comedy of Habit*, p. 62.
[5] *A New and General Biographical Dictionary* (London, 1761), II, 233. *Art.* 'Boerhaave'.
[6] *The World Upside Down* (Oxford, 1970), p. 125.
[7] Introduction to his edition of *The Way of the World* (London, 1971), p. xix.

precise than he is. For them the spectacle of two men being exquisitely polite to each other would have been almost by definition a situation of conflict, and, at the same time, a challenge to discover the nature of this conflict. One would like to know what they made of the very first exchange. As the play opens, Mirabell rises from a game of cards with Fainall in a manner apparently expressing 'coldness'. Fainall hints subtly to him that he is being a bad loser, and Mirabell replies with the suggestion that Fainall has been 'refining on his pleasures'. I suspect that this is meant to convey to the audience that Fainall has been playing dishonestly. It is a point that can hardly be resolved from the dialogue as it stands on the page and yet one that an attentive reader of Congreve should at least register as a possibility. His language needs this kind of scrutiny at all times, and nowhere more than when it is most formal and elegant. There is only the thinnest of barriers between the language of politeness and the language of super-politeness, which is the language of accusation.

The general principle here is one of considerable importance to an understanding of Congreve—namely that conflict is indicated by an increase, not a decrease, in the level of formality. The most exquisitely civil exchange of the play is that between the Fainalls on their first meeting in II.i. and yet there are probably no other characters in the play who hate each other quite so heartily. There is admittedly a level beyond this where nature breaks free of the shackles of art entirely, and outright abuse and even Sir Wilfull's bear-garden flourishes may be in order; but this is relatively rare, and normally signals a fatal loss of control. Thus, to return to the opening exchange between Fainall and Mirabell, it is clear by line ninety or so that they are on quite bad terms with each other. Fainall has been pumping Mirabell about his sham addresses to Lady Wishfort, the first of his plans to secure her consent for the marriage with Millamant. This brings to Mirabell's mind the fact that it was Marwood, Fainall's mistress, who had betrayed the plot. He gently reproaches Fainall with this using the phrase 'your Friend, or your Wife's Friend' to indicate his knowledge of the affair. 'Friend' is deliberately ambiguous here; it can have its neutral modern meaning or it can, as in the *dramatis personae*, be a synonym for mistress. Fainall, appreciating the force of the accusation, tries to find an explanation for Marwood's behaviour that would absolve him of any involvement in the betrayal. With characteristic town suspiciousness and a discernible edge of reproach, he suggests that Marwood would hardly have behaved in such a way if Mirabell

had not given her a reason by rejecting advances from her. Later we
will find that this is also an attempt to probe Mirabell and that Fainall
is distrustful of Marwood and intends to accuse her outright of preferring
Mirabell to himself. Mirabell replies to this clearly and, as far as we
are able to tell, frankly.

> She was always civil to me, till of late; I confess I
> am not one of those Coxcombs who are apt to interpret a
> Woman's good Manners to her Prejudice; and think that
> she who does not refuse 'em every thing, can refuse 'em
> nothing.
>
> [I.i.85–9]

Fainall at this point should have left well alone; instead he proceeds
in a complicated way to call Mirabell a liar. Once again, it is only
later in the play that we will become aware of Fainall's jealousy,
and that his role here is actually that of *curioso impertinente*—the
imaginary cuckold or in this case betrayed lover who will not rest
until he has found proof of his non-existent condition. But for the
moment we will simply note that the language immediately becomes
more formal and that this represents a deliberate indication of hostility
on Fainall's part:

> You are a gallant Man, *Mirabell*; and tho' you may
> have Cruelty enough, not to satisfie a Lady's longing; you
> have too much Generosity, not to be tender of her Honour.
> Yet you speak with an Indifference which seems to be
> affected; and confesses you are conscious of a Negligence.
>
> [I.i.90–4]

The expression here has become so periphrastic that the sense of the
statement is not immediately clear: what matters is the perceptible
freezing and formalizing and the carefully calculated ambiguity of
'negligence', which could either refer to Mirabell's behaviour towards
Marwood or be a euphemism for lie. Clearly Mirabell makes the
second interpretation: his reply to Fainall is even more frozen, more
clotted, and more devoid of readily extractable sense:

> You pursue the Argument with a distrust that seems
> to be unaffected, and confesses you are conscious of a

Concern for which the Lady is more indebted to you, than
your Wife.

[I.i.95–8]

Here the exchange reaches its maximum point of formality, which
is to say of conflict, and it is Fainall who backs down. He accuses
Mirabell of being 'censorious' and leaves the room. When he returns a
minute or so later Mirabell has calmed down a little, or perhaps has
reminded himself of the part Fainall must be induced to play in the
intricate schemes that lie ahead. For the rest of the scene he is prepared
to be perfectly agreeable to him, though not without interpolating
a grave warning against the liberties he permits his wife, who, we
later discover, was formerly 'friend' to Mirabell himself.

The passage just discussed indicates the supreme importance of
verbal nuance in the articulation of dramatic relationships. The basic
point is that the language of the play is the language of politeness
and that the all-important processes of manipulation must take place
through that language. To a certain extent other people can be control-
led through politeness alone: we must presume that Mirabell gains
the support of Mrs. Fainall and Sir Willfull largely through the unaided
power of charm. But appeal may also need to be made to stronger
coercive forces—law, money, sex, even violence—and it is important
that we should not let ourselves be deceived by the bland and allusive
language in which these things are sometimes evoked, into mistaking
the substance of the evocation. A casual exchange between Petulant
and Mirabell in Act I brings out a joking threat of violence which
is far from being as innocent as it seems. 'Have you not left off your
impudent Pretensions there yet?' Mirabell asks on hearing from Fainall
that Petulant is still paying court to Millamant, 'I shall cut your Throat,
sometime or other, *Petulant*, about that Business.' The remark is
dropped quite casually into a good-humoured enough conversation
and yet is clearly meant to have a dissuasive force beyond its ostensible
jokiness. Mirabell will not really cut Petulant's throat—Petulant is
not worth such attention—but he would presumably have no qualms
about kicking him, publicly humiliating him, or entangling him in
a trick marriage; nor would he hesitate to challenge and possibly kill
a more considerable interloper. His reply when Petulant attempts a
huff in return is sharper and brings about an immediate retreat:

> *Petulant.* Ay, ay, let that pass———There are other Throats
>   to be cut———

Mirabell. Meaning mine, Sir?
Petulant. Not I———I mean no Body———I know nothing
———But there are Uncles and Nephews in the World
———And they may be Rivals———What then? All's
one for that———

[I.i.425–31]

Petulant's role in the play is to be and remain futile; Fainall's to suffer defeat through the agency of Mirabell. One of the reasons for this, though one which is never explicitly brought out in the dialogue, is that they will not fight. Fainall at the end of the play has received a most hideous humiliation at Mirabell's hands; his response as an injured husband should have been to challenge him, and his sword is indeed drawn, but it is on Mrs. Fainall, not on her paramour. Lady Wishfort has some fears at the end that Fainall may adopt 'some desperate Course', but Mirabell knows his man better: '*Madam, disquiet not your self on that account, to my knowledge his Circumstances are such, he must of force comply.*' Mirabell's sword, though it is neither drawn nor even specifically referred to, is just as important an instrument in bringing the conflict to its resolution as Mrs. Fainall's deed of gift.

III

In the last few pages I have been trying to suggest how the motives of the principal characters in *The Way of the World* may have been interpreted by its first audiences. Stripped of the varnish of politeness, their interactions are for the most part revealed as hard and combative. Yet granted this combativeness and the selfishness which is its root— and Congreve makes no attempt to veil these things—the fact remains that the spectacle taken as a whole is not a disgusting one, that the treatment is comic, not satiric, and that the comedy, by comparison with Jonson's, say, or even that of *The Double Dealer*, is of a remarkably genial and enlivening kind. We saw something similar to this in *Love for Love*, but there we were dealing with what is self-confessedly a holiday play, where evil was disarmed of menace and enormous risks could be run without danger. In *The Way of the World* evil has its weapons in its hands again and is eager to use them. The world is not a holiday world but one in which actions can be expected to produce much the same consequences as they do in the real world and risks can no longer be run with impunity. Despite the spirit of lightheartedness in which the problems are posed, they are genuine ones, and Congreve wants our assent to his solutions to be a genuine one. Critics have always found this disparity between tone and material difficult to take. In the last century it was the fashion to call him 'heartless'; in our own the most favoured term has been 'trivial'. The objection in each case is that the resolutions come too easily, or to borrow a phrase from the malefactor himself, 'If you speak Truth, your endeavouring at Wit is very unseasonable.'

There are, I believe, certain answers which can be made on Congreve's behalf to these charges. In the first place, we need to recognize that although his handling of the problems may not be to our liking, he is just as aware of them as we are, aware of selfishness, aware of callousness, aware of manipulation, and not necessarily approving. We see these things in his play because he has put them there. His concern as a dramatist is with the grounds and consequences of human choice, and he knows that choice is in the majority of cases the effect of pride, appetite and self love. But this does not make him an advocate for these things. Having reached this awareness, two choices are open. One can challenge and in challenging attempt to transcend the limitations of life in the Mandevillean hive, or one can accept them as inevitable, as an unalterable condition of social existence, and turn instead to the problem of how we are best to live with them. Congreve's is the second choice. In the freer atmosphere of *Love for Love* it had been possible to hint at a solution through transcendence, but in *The Way of the World* he has disciplined himself to what is practically attainable in the world as it stands. Given this perspective, the achievement of Mirabell and Millamant is far from despicable. No doubt in the years that lie ahead they will read their Shaftesbury and their Pope and acquire much more elevated notions of benevolence and moral duty, but for the time being it is as much as can be expected that they are capable of affection, honest to themselves about their appetites without being helpless before them, and prepared to protect the interests of others when they are not directly in conflict with their own. In other words their moral perceptions are those of ninety percent of the human beings we have to deal with in the course of our lives. Congreve takes certain things as given, probably pretty much the same things as Mandeville took, and then sets out to discover how much can be achieved on the basis they offer. If we complain that not very much has been achieved, Congreve's answer would no doubt be that there was not very much

available to start with, and that the value of the spectacle is not in
the point to which the characters arrive, but how far and with what
degree of courage and imagination they have travelled. The quality
of the attempt, in other words, matters more than what is accomplished.

These considerations will make clear, I trust, that Congreve's
point of view is ultimately a moral one. As such it is still, of course,
open to moral objections. Are there not conditions when simply
to accept limitations—and the choice of comedy rather than satire
as the means for presenting this world is itself an acceptance of limitations—is to capitulate before life? The Victorians certainly thought
so, and Congreve's most insistent modern critics have implied the
same thing. I feel myself that this notion rests on an over simplifica-
tion and I would like to propose another possible resolution to the
problem. The assumption of the critics is that when we laugh at
Congreve's characters we are laughing at their inadequacies, that
this is too easy a reaction, and that the objects presented deserve a
more searching and serious response than laughter. However, to
say this is to assume that our attitude towards these characters is a
negative and critical one only. I would like to suggest, and will be
developing the idea further in the pages which follow, that there is
another element to them which is positive and affirmative, and that
our laughter, and Congreve's concern to elicit our laughter rather
than our scorn, springs from a recognition of this.

The best place to begin such an enquiry is with Petulant, neither a
villain nor a victim but more than just a stander-by. His is the despon-
dent role of the knowing loser. His manner, as if in calculated defiance
of the world of elaborate politeness which surrounds him, is truculent
and contradictory, but the defiance does not go very deep; it is only
with the insensate Witwoud that he ventures genuine rudeness. With
Mirabell he retreats at the first hint of hostile reaction into mumbled
inconsequentialities. He would like to be a fighter, but fears to fight.
He would like to be a great seducer, and develops elaborate stratagems
to build a reputation as such—paying whores posing as ladies of
virtue to call and ask for him at coffee houses—but the most he ever
arrives at is to go to bed with his maid. If he were a Witwoud, the
reputation would have been sufficient in itself, but Petulant cannot
be satisfied with this, he quite sincerely wants the actual thing. The
reputation is an attempt to get the thing; but one that he knows will
be useless. Possibly he is quite as deeply in love with Millamant as

Mirabell is, and yet his one attempt to approach her is a complete flop: 'Look you Mrs. *Millamant,*—If you can love me dear Nymph—say it—and that's the Conclusion—pass on, or pass off,—that's all.' This is the voice of a man who knows in advance that the answer will be negative (and would probably not have asked the question anyway if he had not happened to be drunk), yet who would at least like to be taken notice of. But Millamant ignores him or perhaps has not even heard him. Where his friend Witwoud, secure in his good opinion of himself, is invulnerably armed against unflattering realities, Petulant sees the world as it is and realizes that he is never going to have the prizes reserved for the Mirabells. At the same time, however, and this is an important element in our response to him, he never ceases to be an aspirer: the fact that his abilities are so absurdly disproportionate to his aspirations is a misfortune, but that he has such visions and, however ineptly, tries to live up to them allows us to classify him among the play's resisters. He is living to the utmost pitch of what he knows and we can respond to the resoluteness of the attempt even when we cannot give much regard to the achievement.

Lady Wishfort shares Petulant's desperate hunger for the prizes and total inability to secure them. She would like ideally to have Mirabell. Since she cannot she will be content for him to be poisoned or reduced to rags. And as, failing Mirabell, any one would be better than no one, she is prepared to replace him with anyone. The result of this is her warm reception of Sir Rowland, who, in addition to having it in his power to disinherit Mirabell, bears with him the reputation of being a 'brisk man'. Ultimately it is not Sir Rowland or even Mirabell she wants but something she can never have—youth, beauty, repute, the power to manage and dominate others. Lacking all hope of securing these she makes do with a lively imagination and the cherry brandy bottle. However, between her and Petulant there is a crucial difference. Where Petulant gazes disheartenedly on the spectacle presented to him by actuality, Lady Wishfort's method is one of heroic confrontation. Where the Mirabells, Millamants, and Fainalls rely for their power on a searching and judicious inquiry into the true nature of things, she is prepared to act on the basis of what reality ought to be. The feigned addresses of Mirabell become a dream of impossible rapture:

> *Lady Wishfort.* O Sir *Rowland,* the hours that he has dy'd
> away at my Feet, the Tears that he has shed, the Oaths

that he has sworn, the Palpitations that he has felt, the
Trances, and the Tremblings, the Ardors and the Ecstacies,
the Kneelings and the Riseings, the Heart-heavings, and the
hand-Gripings, the Pangs and the Pathetick Regards of
his protesting Eyes!

[IV.i.511–17]

Her rages are magnificent. It is not enough to her to curse; her imagination will only be satisfied by violent action, or at least the prospect
of it:

> *Lady Wishfort.* Ods my Life, I'll have him, I'll have him
> murder'd. I'll have him poyson'd. Where does he eat? I'll
> marry a Drawer to have him poyson'd in his Wine. I'll
> send for *Robin* from *Lockets*————Immediately.
>
> [III.i.102–5]

The discovery of Foible's part in the Sir Rowland fiasco brings forth
the most remarkable rhodomontade of all. A whole history conceived
in horrifying detail and embracing the future as well as the past must
be created for the offending party:

> *Lady Wishfort.* Away, out, out, go set up for your self again
> ————do, drive a Trade, do, with your three penny-worth
> of small Ware, flaunting upon a Packthread, under a
> Brandy-sellers Bulk, or against a dead Wall by a Ballad-
> monger. Go hang out an old *Frisoneer-gorget*, with a yard of
> Yellow *Colberteen* again; do; an old gnaw'd *Mask*, two
> rowes of *Pins* and a *Childs Fiddle*; A *Glass Necklace* with the
> Beads broken, and a *Quilted Night-cap* with one Ear. Go,
> go, drive a trade, . . .
>
> [V.i.10–18]

It should not be thought that Lady Wishfort spends her entire
life in a world of prophetic imaginings; nor that her flights when
they do occur are necessarily self-indulgent or arbitrary. Each is
called forth by a particular situation and is in its way an attempt to
rise to the challenge posed by that situation. They are not evasions
but defyings of the actual—taking the threatening fate by the throat
and challenging it to do its worst. The same dogged determination
not to let unwelcome realities get the better of her will be found

even in situations when she cannot deny their existence, as for instance, in her contemplations of her decayed beauties:

> *Foible.* Your Ladyship has frown'd a little too rashly, indeed Madam. There are some Cracks discernable in the white Vernish.
> *Lady Wishfort.* Let me see the Glass——Cracks, say'st thou? Why I am arrantly flea'd——I look like an old peel'd Wall. Thou must repair me *Foible*, before Sir *Rowland* comes; or I shall never keep up to my Picture.
>
> [III.i.144-50]

Despite the grotesqueness of the image, the linguistic act is essentially a positive, asserting one. It is like Foresight's serene acknowledgement of cuckoldry, but in Lady Wishfort's case it goes beyond resignation to a savage rejoicing in the unwelcome, an act of defiance against the realities of the world from out of the deeper reality of felt energies, an assertion that however meagre and absurd the materials of life may be it is still possible to use them creatively. Like Falstaff, she knows her pretensions to the grand and enviable qualities are a fraud, but will defend to the death her right to keep up her pretence that they are not.

At the close of the play, when the revelation of the concealed deed has suddenly, miraculously released her from the trap laid by her son-in-law, she turns to Mrs. Fainall with a rapturous 'O Daughter, Daughter, 'tis plain thou hast inherited thy Mother's prudence.' The moment is magical. No character in the play has shown herself less capable of prudence than Lady Wishfort. Her whole career has been one headlong search for imprudent indulgence at any cost, and yet to give her her due, no character has laboured more heroically after the appearance of prudence. How is she to greet Sir Rowland?

> Will he be Importunate *Foible*, and push? For if he shou'd not be Importunate——I shall never break Decorums——I shall die with Confusion, if I am forc'd to advance——Oh no, I can never advance——I shall swoon if he shou'd expect advances. No, I hope Sir *Rowland* is better bred, than to put a Lady to the necessity of breaking her Forms . . . I have a mortal Terror at the apprehension of offending

against Decorums. Nothing but Importunity can surmount
Decorums. O I'm glad he's a brisk Man.

[III.i.156–62; 177–80]

Prudence on this scale ceases to have any relationship to the paltry
virtue of that name. It is an immense sparring at an impossible but
passionately admired ideal. It has all the Quixotic fervour of Florence
Foster Jenkins's assault on the Queen of the Night's aria from *The
Magic Flute*. Falstaff's pretensions to physical prowess are of the same
order; but, as is also his case, the devotion to the ideal can somehow
coexist with a devastating eye for the main chance. However enticing
the role, it will never get in the way of a proffered immediate grati-
fication, whatever convoluted posturings may be necessary to reconcile
the two. And she is tougher than Falstaff in that she is able to survive
the shattering of her deepest illusion. With Mirabell lost for good, she
is back in the dance.

In looking at Lady Wishfort, I have been trying to lay stress not
on what she stands for in the world of the play, but on the basis of
her appeal to us, which is something altogether different. In the world
of the play she is a figure of fun, a gull to be manœuvred by the
most stale and obvious stratagems, but as a source of comic energies
she is, or should be, our benefactor. Absurdity in her hands becomes
a source of strength; comedy ceases to be an evasion and becomes a
challenge to life. If we can see the play, as I suggested earlier, as
concerned with the problem of how we are to resist the deadening
force of the world whose ways are so searchingly explored, she is one
of the two unquestionable successes. One would hardly wish to share
her predicament *in* that world, her vulgarity, her stupidity, her blindness, but these things are redeemed for us by others, by her immense
powers of resilience, her unquenchable optimism, and the sheer
voracity of her hunger for life. It is certainly better to be a Lady
Wishfort than to be a Marwood, or a Petulant, or a Witwoud, or a
Fainall.

IV

If Lady Wishfort's fate is to aspire greatly but fruitlessly, Millamant's
is to perform effortlessly what Lady Wishfort can only dream about.
Her place in the play is analogous to that of Angelica in *Love for Love*.
Once again the love intrigue embodies the notion of courtship as a

school of civility in which the woman is the instructor and the man the pupil. Millamant's concern is to educate Mirabell to the point where he will be acceptable as a husband, however her demands are not as taxing as Angelica's had been on Valentine. She will be quite content to have him a good husband as the world understands good husbands. She is equally content that their relationship should continue in marriage to have its component of agreeable deceptions and petty insincerities, indeed she specifically insists that it should. They are to be 'very strange and well bred', as strange 'as if we had been married a great while; and as well bred as if we were not marri'd at all' [IV.i. 207-9]. The aim is not to transcend the world, but to make the best that can be made of what the world provides.

At the stage of the process at which we encounter Mirabell he is obviously fairly close to meeting her requirements; however, there are still a number of traits which would clearly be undesirable in a husband. He likes having his own way and is not too scrupulous about how he gets it. There is a certain tendency to over-organize about him which makes him quite unlike the mercurial Valentine: his intrigues against Lady Wishfort are conducted with all the foresight, thoroughness and discipline of a Marlborough campaign. (No doubt it is part of the lesson that they should flop.) There is also a tendency to be what Fainall calls 'censorious' and Millamant 'sententious'.

Millamant's method in endeavouring to cure him of these blemishes is to subject him to a barrage of the opposite qualities—frivolity and unpredictability. Our first description of her comes in his account of the Cabal night when she had deliberately set out to irritate him. Mirabell knows her well enough by now to recognize that everything she does, even the apparently spontaneous things, is perfectly calculated. 'Her Follies,' he has discovered, 'Are so natural, or so artful, that they become her; and those Affectations which in another Woman wou'd be odious, serve but to make her more agreeable' [I.i.160-3]. On their first meeting, which takes place in Act II, he is directly reprimanded for his attempts to restrict her liberty: 'I shan't endure to be reprimanded, nor instructed;' she tells him, ''Tis so dull to act always by Advice, and so tedious to be told of one's Faults . . .' She wonders whether she should have him or not, and lingers tauntingly over the question. When he still insists on being sententious she compares him to '*Solomon* at the dividing of the Child in an old Tapestry-hanging'. He asks her to be serious and she laughs at him. A

Hc

few seconds later she is going to have him after all: '*Mirabell*, If ever
you will win me woe me now—' and then she has vanished, leaving
him in exasperated wonder: 'To think of a Whirlwind, tho' 'twere
in a Whirlwind, were a Case of more steady Contemplation . . .'
[II.i. 491–2].

Mirabell, however, is not always left in such disarray. In the course
of his wooing he has been slowly getting Millamant's measure even
as he has been purging himself of bossiness and ponderous attitudes.
When the moment of agreement finally comes in Act IV it is a meeting
of perfect equals who are ready to give everything that can meaning-
fully be given, but also know what it is essential to keep. Millamant
is to have her liberty to rise when she pleases, and go where she
pleases, absolute sovereignty over her tea table, and the right not to
be affronted by public displays of uxoriousness. Mirabell in return is
permitted to forbid unnecessary playacting, excessive use of cosmetics,
straight lacing during pregnancy and secret tippling with women
friends. This justly admired scene also represents a final harmonizing
of the three contradictory pressures of affection, kinship and law. It
is couched as a series of secret clauses to the formal marriage contract
which is to establish a new dynastic relationship, that, unlike most
of the others we have seen in Congreve, will be firmly grounded
in affection. However, as the very use of the proviso formula makes
clear, this harmony is not providential or fortuitious, but something
that comes from mutual respect and a readiness to compromise. There
is nothing sentimental about it. A marriage undertaken on these
principles will not, as I said before, be a break with the ways of the
world, but an attempt to put these ways to the best use that can be
found for them.

In his last comedy Congreve's sights are set lower than they had been
in *Love for Love* or *The Double Dealer*. It seems to me nonetheless,
and I hope the argument will not smack too much of special pleading,
that to restrict one's consideration to the critical and satiric aspects of
the play—the vision of a world in which only a restricted range of
human possibilities can be allowed realization—is to omit something
which is equally vital to its effect as a work of art. I would suggest
again that Congreve wants us to recognize that nearly all his characters
are attempting in one way or another, successfully and unsuccessfully,
knowledgeably and ignorantly, to resist the restrictions. On a wider
scale comedy itself may even be seen as a form of resistance. In the
case of Lady Wishfort, the limitations of resource are redeemed by a

grandeur of aspiration, and our fundamental response is to the grandeur, not the limitations. In Millamant's case and Mirabell's the resources, though much richer, are still restricted by comparison with those of Shakespeare's Berowne and Rosaline, or Shirley's Celestina and Lord A. What redeems them is our awareness that those possibilities that *were* available to them have been developed to their utmost point of perfection, and that, as with Lady Wishfort, the values exhibited in the endeavour are just as relevant to our appraisal as the substance of what is humanly achieved.

6

Some Dissenters

It would be disingenuous of me to end this account of the comedies without reference to a body of dissenters who would deny that Congreve is a great dramatist, and in one or two cases even that he is a major dramatist. To present a formal exposition and critique of their views would be out of keeping with the scale of the present study so my aim must simply be to summarize the opinions of the hostile critics as economically as is consistent with intelligibility and to indicate some of the reasons why I do not myself find these opinions of weight. Any further enquiry must be made of the critics themselves, who, for the most part, will amply repay it. The battle royal over Restoration comedy, which has been one of the hardest fought of literary *causes célèbres*, has also been highly fortunate in the quality of its contestants.

The traditional objection to the plays was a moralistic one deriving from their failure to observe a number of theatrical taboos which came into force with the generation immediately following Congreve's and were to remain influential until about the twenties of our own century. The nature of these will be evident from the bill of complaints presented against the Restoration dramatists and the persons of their dramas by Jeremy Collier—'Cursing and Swearing', 'downright Blasphemy', 'The Clergy abused by the Stage', 'The Stage-Poets make Libertines their Top-Characters, and give them Success in their Debauchery', 'Course Usage of the Nobility'.[1] These were also substantially the charges brought by Dr. Johnson in his life of Congreve and by Lord Macaulay in his famous *Edinburgh Review* essay

[1] Jeremy Collier, *A Short View of the Immorality and Profaneness of the English Stage*, 3rd edn. (London, 1698), A4ᵛ–A6ʳ *passim*.

of 1841, the latter occasioned by attempts to rehabilitate the dramatists on the part of Lamb, Hazlitt and Leigh Hunt. The social and critical issues underlying this phase of the debate have been well analysed in a recent essay by Andrew Bear.[2]

By the 1930s the evolution of public attitudes had removed most of the ostensible grounds of disapproval; however, as if to show that the real objections had always lain deeper than this, the same decade saw the moralistic critique restated in new and much more testing ways. The most influential of the dissenting voices has been that of L. C. Knights, whose 'Restoration Comedy, the Reality and the Myth' is now approaching its fortieth birthday.[3] The essay begins by proposing two yardsticks against which the achievement of the Restoration dramatists may be measured—the social comedy of Henry James, as the standard of 'maturity', and Elizabethan drama, in which Knights finds a variety of interests, a rich common language, and a living relationship with the broader culture of the time that he feels to be lacking in the comedy of Congreve and his immediate predecessors. The heart of his paper is an attack on the language of the comedies as failing to achieve 'a genuinely sensitive and individual mode of expression' [p. 9] and inhibiting 'any but the narrowest— and the most devastatingly *expected*—response'. This he sees as reflecting a fundamental poverty of attitudes, the stock assumptions turning up 'with the stale monotony of jokes on postcards' and requiring 'only the easiest, the most superficial, response' [p. 14]. Of Congreve in particular he has this to say:

> Even Congreve, by common account the best of the comic writers, is no exception. I have said that his verbal pattern often seems to be quite unrelated to an individual mode of perceiving. At best it registers a very limited mode. Restoration prose is all 'social' in its tone, implications and general tenor, but Congreve's observation is *merely* of the public surface. And Congreve, too, relies on the conventional assumptions. In *The Way of the World*, it is true, they are mainly given to the bad and the foolish to express: it is Fainall who discourses on the pleasures

[2] Andrew Bear. 'Restoration Comedy and the Provok'd Critic' in *Restoration Literature: Critical Approaches*, ed. Harold Love (London: Methuen, 1972), pp. 1–26.

[3] L. C. Knights, 'Restoration Comedy, the Reality and the Myth', *Scrutiny* VI (1937), 122–43. Also in his *Explorations* (1946), pp. 131–49, and in John Loftis's *Restoration Drama, Modern Essays in Criticism* (New York, 1966), pp. 3–21. Page references are to Loftis.

of disliking one's wife, and Witwoud who maintains that only old age and ugliness ensure constancy. And Mirabell, who is explicitly opposed to some aspects of contemporary manners, goes through the common forms in a tone of rather weary aloofness: 'I wonder, Fainall, that you who are married, and of consequence should be discreet, will suffer your wife to be of such a party.' But Congreve himself is not above raising a cheap snigger; and, above all, the characters with some life in them have nothing to fall back on—nothing, that is, except the conventional, and conventionally limited, pleasures of sex.

[pp. 15–16]

The terms of this denunciation are severe ones, and have governed the course of most subsequent debate over the worth of the comedies.

A more elaborate attempt to develop a critique along the lines indicated in Knights's essay is D. R. M. Wilkinson's *The Comedy of Habit*, published in 1964, a serious and well-documented book which deserves much more careful consideration than it has received to date or than it can be given here. Wilkinson accepts Knights's analysis of the stock assumptions of Restoration drama and is able to give it historical perspective from a study of the way in which the Restoration wit and gallant is presented in contemporary courtesy books and works of popular devotion. This material allows him to bring out very clearly how limited and formulaic the basic moves of the wit game are—indeed his book provides the basis for a very useful terminology to describe these moves—and how narrow and egotistic is the wits' vision of life. He sees a continuity in attitudes between the cynical realism current during the Cromwellian years and the social mistrust of the wits; however, he also feels that these attitudes do not have the same pressure of experience behind them in the comedies as they do in his favourite among the courtesy writers (if this is not to overstrain the term), Francis Osborne:

It can be shown, no doubt, that Osborne and the playwrights shared certain convictions about the nature of social man— that a persevering reliance on his good will is the mark of a fool: that he is an untrustworthy, even treacherous, animal; that a certain discipline of suspicion is necessary in treating with him; and that there is little connection, in this world, between appearances and the underlying realities. They tend to agree, in fact, that distrust is a kind of virtue. Such a correlation of viewpoints,

however, is meaningless if the spirit in which the beliefs are
held, and the form in which they are expressed, are not taken
into account. . . . If the playwrights may be said to have shared
Osborne's convictions, they seem to have lacked the experience
that gave rise to them, and gave point to them in Osborne.

[pp. 33–4]

Wilkinson also stresses the prominence given to fear of ridicule as a
factor governing behaviour in the world presented by the dramatists
and the restrictions this fear places on personal expression; yet he
will not accept that the dramatists are aware of the restrictions or that
their vision of social man is dramatically placed and appraised. The
'sense of comic distrust' seems to him to be 'grounded in habit rather
than any relevant need' [p. 34] and it is ultimately in a craven compliance
with the demands and expectations of an audience of 'gallants' that
he finds the dominant motivation of the Restoration dramatist.

The most recent attack on Congreve's reputation comes in George
Parfitt's 'The Case against Congreve' read to the Leeds tri-centenary
conference in 1970.[4] Where Knights and Wilkinson had been concerned with the values implicit in the language and artistic methods
of the Restoration dramatists quite as much as with what was actually
shown and stated in their plays, Parfitt has chosen to concentrate
more narrowly, and perhaps a little old-fashionedly, on the attitudes
exhibited by the characters, and the question of how far these attitudes
can be held to have Congreve's considered approval. His basic objection to Congreve is exactly that of Angelica's words to Jeremy in
Love for Love which I have already quoted in a similar context: 'If you
speak Truth, your endeavouring at Wit is very unseasonable—.' He
is disturbed that Congreve does not take seriously or does not appear
to take seriously a number of things that a modern reader might be
expected to take very seriously indeed, among them Mirabell's
apparent callousness towards Mrs. Fainall, the abused honesty of
Ben, and Valentine's joke about infanticide (though here I think he
is simply missing the 'quizzical' tone of the whole exchange from which
the line comes). He is also worried about what he feels to be a lack of
connection between realistically conceived and 'formal demonstrative'
elements in the plays, and inconsistencies in characterization.

If we respond with any seriousness at all to *The Old Batchelour*
it is difficult to avoid the feeling that Congreve fails to register

[4] In Brian Morris, ed., *William Congreve* (London, 1972), pp. 23–38.

Bellmour's seduction of Sylvia adequately . . . Miss Lynch
tries to ease this odd distinction by calling Sylvia 'a designing
courtesan', but when we first see her she seems—if we read the
text rather than 'typing' the figure almost before its appearance
—a rather pathetically wronged individual, only unwillingly
the deceiver of Heartwell. If she is a wronged figure does she
deserve the wretched Wittol? If she is Miss Lynch's designing
courtesan does even Wittol, who is foolish rather than vicious,
deserve her? In either case, does Bellmour deserve his reward
by comparison?   [p. 26]

Parfitt is in general agreement with Knights and Wilkinson that
'the world of the comedies is very limited, its values thin, uncertain,
confused, its view of character sometimes unclear' but unlike them is
prepared to question the appropriateness of the criteria by which
such judgements have been made. He recognizes that these things
are not in themselves a sufficient basis for condemnation 'because one
has not yet defined what his comedies seem to be trying to do and
what the authorial attitude is' [p. 31]. He goes on from this statement
to investigate various possibilities in turn. Consideration is given to
an 'art for art's sake approach', a 'way things are' approach, a 'realist'
approach (as developed in T. H. Fujimura's *The Restoration Comedy
of Wit*), a 'satirico-moral' approach and 'a final line of defence, according to which Congreve is not only aware of the weaknesses of his
Truewits but also aware of how limited even their lives and aspirations are', an approach which Parfitt feels obliged to reject on the
grounds which were his original reason for dissatisfaction with Congreve—that it does not allow us to bridge such disparities as 'the odd
gap in Mirabell between his love for Millamant and his inability to
feel for Mrs. Fainall'. Finding that none of his keys fit, he concludes
that despite the fact that the last two comedies 'can provide a splendid
evening at the theatre', Congreve's limitation 'is finally that his
vision is neither large enough nor sufficiently clear to be really satisfying' [p. 37].

* * *

What has gone before in this book will have indicated a number
of points at which I am in quite fundamental disagreement with the
readings and interpretations proposed by Knights, Wilkinson and
Parfitt. Indeed, I am forced to confess that I find subtlety where they
find banality, largeness where they find limitation, and clarity where

they find evasion, and that Parfitt's 'last line of defence' would be for me the natural and obvious response to the plays of any reader or theatregoer sensitive to dramatic values. Moreover, I feel strongly that whatever Congreve's faults (and I would not want to claim he is a Jonson or a Chekhov), he is still big enough to trust—in other words that we should be prepared to let meanings grow out of the text without requiring that the dramatist be somehow 'proved' to have intended them.

This is clearly not the view of the three hostile critics. Knights, Wilkinson and Parfitt conceive their critical role quite explicitly as that of guardians of the canon, literary immigration officers confronted with a suspicious stranger. With Parfitt, however, one at least feels that he has taken the trouble to look the stranger in the face. I am aware that his plays are recognizably my plays, and can appreciate how if approached under certain assumptions which are not my own they could give occasion for his judgements. Knights and Wilkinson, I am sorry to say, do not inspire me with this kind of confidence; in fact, I find it difficult to believe at times that we can all have been reading the same words. (This is not as silly as it sounds. There are still numerous copies of barbarously mangled eighteenth century acting versions of Restoration plays lying around and at least one of these has found its way into a widely circulated paperback.) But what on earth is one to think of a critic who can find no more to interest or engage him in *The Way of the World* than this?—

> There is perhaps more variety in the repartee than in the earlier Restoration comedies, and the level of it is higher. The laugh is thus earned more frequently; but in this case it is also earned more blatantly at the expense of the plot, whose complications add little of importance, and tend to weary the attention without rewarding it. The vaunted intelligence of Mirabell and Milla-mant seems to reside in nothing more satisfactory than their capacities for threading their ways successfully and convention-ally through these complications.   [p. 165]

That Wilkinson could write in these terms of the play is as puzzling to me as that Thomas Rymer could say of *Othello* that 'The *Characters* or Manners . . . are not less unnatural and improper than the Fable was improbable and absurd.'[5] And as with Rymer it is not really possible to argue; one can only contradict.

---

[5] *The Critical Works of Thomas Rymer*, ed. Curt A. Zimansky (New Haven, 1956), p. 134.

The charge that I am compelled to bring against Knights and Wilkinson is that they came to their critical conclusions after and not before the formulation of a general thesis about the plays and have failed as a consequence to register them adequately as works of art. In Knights's case this is almost flaunted. The reader is left in no doubt that the obligation to scan through a representative selection of Restoration plays has been a tiresome distraction from more important matters and that the height of his concern was to assemble evidence which would enable him to challenge a view of them advanced by certain of their admirers. In challenging this view he is, of course, brilliantly successful, but successful, I would like to suggest, as a rhetorician, not as a critic. His paper has all the tightness, incisiveness and telling modulations of tone we would expect from a good satire, and yet the writer to whom Vanbrugh's *The Relapse* is a source of 'unmitigated fatigue' to be lumped indiscriminately with the inanities of *Sir Martin Mar-all* [p. 3] can hardly complain if his readers choose to doubt either his seriousness or the extent of his acquaintance with the thing he criticizes.

In Wilkinson's case the general thesis is a historical one and is advanced with an eloquent earnestness which unfortunately fails to compensate for a serious flaw in its logic. He is able to establish entirely valid similarities between the gallants of his courtesy books and the young men of the comedies; but then expects us to assume with him that Restoration drama was written for an *audience* composed of such gallants, an assumption which has no historical justification whatsoever and forces him into a position where he has to put the worst possible interpretation on everything the plays have to offer. *The Way of the World*, we are told, can be allowed to be 'no better than the "Manners" convention permits', by which he means that it can be allowed to suggest nothing that is not measured to the capacity of a gallant as determined for us by writers of works of moral instruction. Here Wilkinson reveals himself as a victim, and probably not the last, of a myth of the Restoration audience originally set in circulation by Jeremy Collier and his clerical accomplices and which is unlikely to have been any closer to the truth than the average British TV viewer's impression of the prevalence of violent crime in the streets of New York.

Wilkinson must also be charged with a total lack of sensitivity to theatrical effect and the integrity of the dramatic mode. His comparison is one which proceeds from the courtesy books to the plays and which ranks the plays according to the extent to which they show themselves capable of performing the functions of a courtesy book. Knights is guilty of much the same kind of distortion. He reads and judges the comedies exactly as if they were novels in dialogue, and, despite his genuflection to the Elizabethans, it is the aesthetic of the novel, as exemplified by Flaubert and Henry James, which provides his ultimate standard of judgement. Knights's two basic assumptions—that the language of a work of literature should embody a 'an individual mode of perceiving' and its obverse that the author should eschew the predictable attitude and the stock response—are indeed central to the aims of the novel, especially of the nineteenth century novel, but it is not shown why they should be as crucial to the evaluation of stage comedy. His governing paradigm is one of a single self-realizing creator, an isolated reflective reader, and a realistically portrayed, immaculately ordered 'world'. Parfitt's basic assumptions are much the same. He wants characters who are single and unambiguous and an author who has a consistent and definable point of view; he deplores confusions and ambiguities of level; he wants to know precisely where 'Congreve' is and precisely when and how the reader is expected to jump at the authorial bidding; he would not presumably find meaning in the proposition that he might share the experience of the work with other individuals with contradictory needs and interests. Once again his are perfectly sensible expectations to bring to the reading of a novel—indeed they almost add up to a definition of the novel as it is classically conceived—but a novel is not a play and the nineteenth century is not the seventeenth. Drama, after all, comes into existence as a public object in a public space, and at the focus of an intricate pattern of social relationships. As such it must surely be considered deserving of an aesthetic of its own in which terms such as 'author', 'character' and 'point of view' might conceivably have a different kind of artistic substance. These considerations are not in themselves a defence against the charges brought by the three critics, but they do suggest that the demands made on the plays in the first place may easily have been irrelevant ones.

If we are not to approach plays as if they were novels without descriptions, how are we then to go about it? As a first stage it would seem essential that we should acquire some notion of the vocabulary of drama, by which I mean not only the verbal part of that vocabulary but the whole range of expressive devices on which a dramatist can call to communicate meaning—the language of the body, and the scene, as well as that of the tongue, and beyond this the meta-language of social implication (remembering that the theatre itself is also a society). By comparison with most writers of comedy, Congreve has an exceptionally high respect for words and pays exceptionally careful attention to them, yet this does not mean that he is not aware of the principle that the verbal in the theatre is at all points open to qualification from the visual or that he does not mean his performers to introduce such qualifications when they appear necessary. To bring an imagination unschooled in the application of this principle to the reading of a play is to put oneself in the position of a colour-blind man discussing painting or a tone-deaf man music.

A second requirement for a critical approach to the study of a dramatic text is that the critic should be aware of the very special conditions governing the nature and form of the theatrical statement and the special responsibilities these place on the reader. A basic assumption underlying the aesthetic of the novel is that its language should be samplable, in other words that the critic is entitled to select a number of discrete details and make statements on the basis of these about the value of the work as a whole and the mental and moral state of those who wrote and those who admired it. What such a view overlooks is that a play is never a single homogeneous discourse but makes use of a bold and intricate form of shorthand in which apparently equivalent details may be performing entirely different tasks. Parfitt uses a significant phrase when he criticizes Congreve for not 'writing out his play in full' but if he had it would have been five hundred pages long and run for twenty-four hours. Drama, in other words, is under a continual necessity to encode, to compress, to allude, to emblematize, and to make one element serve a multitude of functions.

Today's theatre, partly under the influence of cinema techniques, has made us acutely aware of the nature of this dramatic shorthand; a play by Pinter or Beckett may expect us without any overt guidance from the author to recognize that some things said are realistic and some symbolic, some subjective and some objective, some past, some present and some future, or that in another context nothing as precise as this is intended, and we are simply to register a simultaneity of possibilities. Congreve's shorthand is neither as puzzling nor as radical as this, but it is a shorthand nonetheless, and the demand that the plays remain on a single representational level or present a consistent fullness of realization is one that betrays a basic misunderstanding of the theatrical medium. To criticize Lucy in *The Old Batchelour* or Angelica in *Love for Love* on the grounds of inconsistency is to commit an error of the same order as to criticize the opening scene of Lear on the grounds of psychological implausibility. These 'inconsistencies' are so far from being problems that they are givens—things we start from. The dramatist must move as quickly as he can to what he sees as the essential task, which for Congreve is not in any case a Jamesian or Flaubertian task.

A good play will have a literary existence which is quite independent of its theatrical existence and will ideally be a richer thing than any particular theatrical realization because a reader has the text under direct imaginative control in a way which is impossible for him as a member of an audience; but such a literary existence will be a poor thing indeed if it fails to take account of the special kinds of definition which the text can only receive in performance. The attitude of Knights, Wilkinson and Parfitt would seem on the face of it to be that the theatre has little to offer to an understanding or assessment of Congreve. I have already quoted Parfitt's comment that while *The Way of the World* and *Love for Love* can provide 'a splendid evening at the theatre' Congreve's vision is 'neither large enough nor sufficiently clear to be really satisfying' [p. 37]. Earlier, Knights, after gravely inspecting the behaviour of the audience at a Restoration play, had complained that 'One has only to note the laughter of a contemporary audience at a revival, and the places where the splutters occur, to realize how much of the fun provides a rather gross example of tendency wit' [p. 14]. Wilkinson is prepared to concede that 'It is likely that Congreve's fair popularity on the stage will continue' but is quick to stress that this is 'a fact that has not a great deal to do with the question of his dramatic excellence' [p. 165]. It is not clear how much weight we can fairly lay on these remarks but there is at least a suggestion that the problem with the critics is not merely one of blindness to theatrical values, but extends to a contempt for the theatre itself.

If this is true it is a pity, for it is in the theatre that we are going to find the clearest evidence for Congreve's stature, not merely as an inspirer of splendid and occasionally not so splendid evenings, but, along with Pope and Swift, as one of the three supreme masters of language of his generation. A bad play may be made to look like a good play when it is acted by good actors, but it will rarely survive those actors, or if it does, will survive as a fossil to be reproduced by subsequent casts exactly as bequeathed to them by their predecessors.

The test of a good play is that new generations of performers and theatregoers can come to it and continue to find fresh things in it—that it continues to produce reactions, not just reflexes. Judged by this standard, Congreve's two mature comedies can claim something much more substantial than 'fair popularity on the stage'. Written for Betterton, Barry and Bracegirdle, they passed from them to Booth, Wilks and Oldfield, next to Ryan, Quin and Mrs. Younger and then to Milward, Macklin, Giffard, Kitty Clive, Peg Woffington, Garrick and Mrs. Pritchard. At the turn of the eighteenth century they had reached the very able hands of Kemble and Mrs. Jordan, and as late as 1842 were still to be seen in major productions at Drury Lane and the Haymarket. When they eventually disappeared from the repertoire it was not through any feeling that their dramatic possibilities were exhausted but as a casualty of middle-class moralism. Such men as Byron, Lamb, Hazlitt, and Leigh Hunt lamented their passing, and as soon as the moral taboos began to lose their force, the comedies were at once restored to the stage, beginning with performances for theatre clubs (of which the first was as early as 1904), later in productions mounted by commerical managements and repertory companies, and most recently as a special concern of the National Theatre. The story of Congreve's fortunes on the English stage in the twentieth century has been admirably recounted by Kenneth Muir[6] and need not be repeated here, but it is certainly not a history of fossilization.

When we go to see a lesser comedy of manners such as *The Recruiting Officer* or *The School for Scandal* we will not journey in the expectation of being surprised. These are plays about conventional and predictable characters who act towards each other in conventional, predictable and immediately comprehensible ways. The plays may be well done or badly done; there may be a greater or lesser amount of theatrical imagination applied to them; but their limits have already been probed and fixed for us, and a producer can only go beyond those limits by adding meanings of his own which were not there in the work as he received it. We return to them in order to re-live a pleasant experience rather than to embark on a new one. In Congreve's case the situation is, or should be, very different. He presents us with characters who, while lacking a Shakespearean fullness of life, possess an authentic dramatic individuality and who are placed in relationships with each other which, as the dramatist matures, are increasingly informed with the ambiguities, indeterminacies and conflicting per-

[6] See Kenneth Muir, 'Congreve on the Modern Stage' in Morris, pp. 133–54.

spectives of real life. In the case of a Mirabell, it is not only his attitude to Millamant that concerns us (as would almost certainly have been the case had the play been written by a Sheridan or a Farquhar) but how he stands in relationship to Fainall, Mrs. Fainall, Lady Wishfort, Petulant and Witwoud and how they stand with regard to Mirabell, and to each other. Our view of the play is ultimately one of a pattern of relationships whose elements are continually in motion, and require other elements to answer their motion.

To say this is perhaps to concede Knights's point that Congreve's speech 'is all "social" in its tone, implications and general tenor', but it is certainly not to concede his other claim that the observation is *merely* of the public surface'. The real nature of the social relationships will only be understood when we have penetrated beyond the public surface, beyond the language of deportment, to the appetites and vulnerabilities which that language, and the code of behaviour of which it is part, are expressedly designed to conceal. This does not relieve the performer of the obligation to realize the self-disguising outer manner and to endue the wonderful language with the deceptive simplicity of a Mozart first violin part: that the real nature of the interactions should be so carefully disguised is the essence of the drama (and a Mozart symphony, after all, is much more than a first violin part). What it does mean is that it is possible in performance to generate a sense of society, a sense that what is happening between the characters is just as important as what is happening in them, and that there is not just one but a number of personal perspectives involved, each suggesting its own interpretations and evaluations. The production which can create this sense of society will have created something that will shift and grow from performance to performance and will never be seen by any two audiences in quite the same way. To this extent, at least, the best of Congreve is inexhaustible.

Chronology

Information chiefly from John C. Hodges, *William Congreve the Man*

1670   (24 January) Congreve born at Bardsey, Yorkshire.
1672   Dryden's *Marriage à la Mode*.
1674   William Congreve snr. appointed lieutenant in a company of foot stationed at Youghal, Ireland.
1675   Wycherley's *The Country Wife*.
1676   Etherege's *The Man of Mode* and Wycherley's *The Plain Dealer*.
1677   Dryden's *All for Love*.
1678   The Congreves move to Carrickfergus.
1679   Death of Hobbes.
1678–82 'Popish Plot' and Exclusion Bill crises.
1680   Lee's *Lucius Junius Brutus*.
1681   The Congreves move to Kilkenny.
        Dryden's *Absalom and Achitophel*.
1682   Otway's *Venice Preserv'd*.
        Congreve a pupil at Kilkenny school.
        Amalgamation of the former King's and Duke's companies.
1685   Death of Charles II; accession of James II.
1686–8 Congreve a student at Trinity College Dublin.
1688   Flight of James II; accession of William and Mary.
        Jacobite uprisings in Ireland.
        The Congreves return to England.
        Dryden deprived of laureateship.
1689   The Battle of the Boyne.
        Congreve ill; *The Old Batchelour* drafted.
1691   (17 March) Congreve entered at the Middle Temple.
        Colonel Congreve agent in Ireland for the Earl of Burlington.

1691   (22 December) *Incognita: or Love and Duty Reconcil'd* licensed for publication.
Death of Etherege.

1692   (October) Dryden's *The Satires of Decimus Junius Juvenalis* published, including Congreve's translation of the eleventh satire.
Death of Lee.

1693   (February) Southerne's *The Maid's Last Prayer* with song by Congreve.
(March) First performance of *The Old Batchelour.*
(October?) First performance of *The Double Dealer.*

1694   (28 December) Death of Queen Mary.
Southerne's *The Fatal Marriage.*

1695   Congreve's *The Mourning Muse of Alexis* rewarded with gift of £100 from King William.
(25 March) Royal licence for new theatre at Lincoln's Inn Fields issued.
(30 April) New theatre opens with *Love for Love.*
Congreve one of six Commissioners for Licensing Hackney Coaches.

1696   (19 February) Congreve and Southerne receive M.A.'s from Trinity.

1697   (27 February) First production of *The Mourning Bride.*
Vanbrugh's *The Provoked Wife.*

1698   (April) Jeremy Collier's *A Short View of the Immorality and Profaneness of the English Stage* published.
(July) Congreve's *Amendments of Mr. Collier's False and Imperfect Citations.*

1700   (March) *The Way of the World* performed but with only moderate success.
(1 May) Death of Dryden.
Congreve visits Belgium and Holland.

1701   *The Judgement of Paris* performed in separate settings by Finger, Weldon, Daniel Purcell and John Eccles.

1702   Death of William III; accession of Anne.

1703–5   Congreve involved with Vanbrugh in building a new theatre in the Haymarket.

1704   Contributed to *Squire Trelooby,* a group translation of *Monsieur de Porceaugnac.*
Swift's *A Tale of a Tub.*

1705	Congreve a Commissioner for Wines.
1706	Farquhar's *The Recruiting Officer*.
1708	Farquhar's *The Beaux' Stratagem*. Death of Farquhar. Fielding born. Congreve involved with Swift in the Bickerstaff hoax. Reuniting of the companies.
1709	Wilks, Dogget, and Cibber joint managers at Drury Lane.
1710	(28 April) Death of Betterton. Decline of the Whigs. Congreve apprehensive of losing his posts. Complete edition of his works published by Tonson.
1713	Treaty of Utrecht. (7 November) Death of Elizabeth Barry.
1714	Accession of George I. Congreve appointed Secretary to the Island of Jamaica.
1715	(May) Pope's *Iliad* published with dedication to Congreve.
1717	(19 February) Garrick born.
1722	Visit to Bath with Henrietta Duchess of Marlborough.
1723	Lady Mary Godolphin born; suspected of being Congreve's daughter.
1726	Congreve visited by Voltaire. Ill with 'fever and the gout in his stomach'.
1728	Congreve at Bath with the Duchess of Marlborough. Injured in coach accident.
1729	(19 January) Death of Congreve. (26 January) Buried in Westminster Abbey 'with the usual Pomp and Solemnity'.

Select Bibliography

(i) *Editions*

The best modern editions of the plays are those of F. W. Bateson (1930) and Herbert Davis (1966). A new edition by D. F. McKenzie has been promised. There are separate editions of *The Way of the World* by Kathleen Lynch (1965), A. Norman Jeffares (1966), Brian Gibbons (1971), and John Barnard (1972) and of *Love for Love* by Emmett L. Avery (1966), A. Norman Jeffares (1967), and M. M. Kelsall (1969).

(ii) *General Studies containing Material on Congreve*

Birdsall, Virginia O., *Wild Civility*. Bloomington, 1970.

Dobrée, Bonamy, *Restoration Comedy: 1660–1720*. Oxford, 1924.

Fujimura, T. H., *The Restoration Comedy of Wit*. Princeton, 1952.

Holland, Norman. N., *The First Modern Comedies*. Cambridge, U.S.A., 1959. The most influential of recent studies.

Loftis, John, *Comedy and Society from Congreve to Fielding*. Stanford, 1959.

Lynch, Kathleen M., *The Social Mode of Restoration Comedy*. New York, 1926. With Palmer's and Dobrée's, the most valuable of the earlier studies.

Muir, Kenneth, *The Comedy of Manners*. London, 1970.

Palmer, John, *The Comedy of Manners*. London, 1913.

Schneider, Ben Ross Jnr., *The Ethos of Restoration Comedy*. Urbana, 1971.

Smith, John Harrington, *The Gay Couple in Restoration Comedy*. Cambridge, U.S.A., 1948.

Sutherland, James, *English Literature of the Late Seventeenth Century*. Oxford, 1969. Oxford History of English Literature, Vol. VI.

(iii) *Collections of Shorter Pieces*

Brown, John Russell, and Harris, Bernard, eds., *Restoration Theatre*. London, 1965. Stratford-upon-Avon studies VI. Contains Kenneth Muir's 'The Comedies of William Congreve'.

Loftis, John, ed., *Restoration Drama: Modern Essays in Criticism*. New York, 1966. Includes L. C. Knights's 'Restoration Comedy: The Reality and the Myth' and Clifford Leech's 'Congreve and the Century's End' and 'Restoration Tragedy: A Reconsideration'.

Love, Harold, ed., *Restoration Literature: Critical Approaches*. London, 1972. Contains chapters by Andrew Bear on the debate over Restoration comedy, Philip Parsons on the theatrical aspects of the heroic play, and R. J. Jordan on the 'extravagant rake' as a character type.

Miner, Earl, ed., *Restoration Dramatists: A Collection of Critical Essays*. Englewood Cliffs, 1966. Twentieth Century Views series.

Morris, Brian, ed., *William Congreve*. London, 1972. Mermaid Critical Commentaries. The proceedings of the 1970 tri-centenary conference at the University of York. Includes especially good papers by Malcolm Kelsall, John Barnard and R. A. Foakes.

(iv) *Restoration Theatres and Audiences*

Avery, Emmett, L., Scouten, Arthur H. et al., eds., *The London Stage 1660–1800*. 11 vols. Carbondale, 1960–8.

Cibber, Colley, *An Apology for the Life of Colley Cibber*. London, 1740. Much reprinted and still the most direct route back to the green rooms of the 1690s.

Mullin, Donald C., *The Development of the Playhouse*. Berkeley, 1970.

Nicoll, Allardyce, *History of the English Drama, 1660–1900*, vol. I, *Restoration Drama, 1660–1700*. 4th edn. Cambridge, 1952. Must now be considered out of date.

Wilson, John H., *All the King's Ladies*. Chicago, 1958.

The problem of the Restoration audience was debated by the author and Andrew Bear in *Komos* I (1968), 49–56 and II (1969–70), 23–31 and 72–80.

(v) *On Congreve alone*

Dobrée, Bonamy, *William Congreve*. London, 1963. Writers and their Work, 164.

Hodges, John C., *William Congreve, the Man*. New York, 1941.
William Congreve: Letters and Documents. London, 1964.
The two basic biographical sources.

Lynch, Kathleen M., *A Congreve Gallery*. Cambridge, U.S.A., 1951.

Mueschke, Paul and Miriam, *A New View of Congreve's Way of the World*. Ann Arbor, 1958.

Novak, Maxmilian E., *William Congreve*. New York, 1971. Twayne's English Authors Series.

Taylor, D. Crane, *William Congreve*. Oxford, 1931.

Van Voris, W. H., *The Cultivated Stance: The Designs of Congreve's Plays*. Dublin, 1965.

(vi) *The Case against Congreve*

Bear, Andrew, 'Restoration Comedy and the Provok'd Critic' in Love, *Restoration Literature: Critical Approaches*, pp. 1–26.

Knights, L. C., 'Restoration Comedy: The Reality and the Myth' *Scrutiny* VI (1937), 122–43. Reprinted in *Explorations* (London, 1946), pp. 131–49, and Loftis, *Restoration Drama: Modern Essays in Criticism*, pp. 3–21.

Krutch, Joseph W., *Comedy and Conscience after the Restoration*. rev. edn., New York, 1949.

Parfitt, George, 'The Case against Congreve' in Morris, *William Congreve*, pp. 23–38.

Wilkinson, D. R. M., *The Comedy of Habit*. Leiden, 1964.